# SPARK YOUR INFLUENCE

Inspiring Women to Lead with
Boldness, Purpose, and Passion

MISTY PHILLIP

# Praise, Reviews, Testimonials

"*Spark Your Influence* is a timely call for Christian women to lead with faith and courage. Misty Phillip offers biblical wisdom and practical steps to integrate faith and leadership, making this a vital resource for those pursuing excellence and purpose in a world that challenges biblical values."

~ **Jordan Raynor**
*Author of The Sacredness of Secular Work
and Redeeming Your Time*

"In *Spark Your Influence* Misty Phillip calls women back to God's original design, dismantling the lie that leadership has to come at the cost of peace and family. She beautifully weaves biblical principles with practical steps to help women lead without fear, without burnout, and without compromise."

~ **Sam Sorbo**
*Actress/Author/Speaker*

"God calls women to be influencers for His Kingdom, and *Spark Your Influence* is the guidebook to help you do just that. Misty Phillip blends scriptural truth with practical wisdom to help women embrace leadership with grace, courage, and conviction. This book is a must-read for women who feel called to lead but need the confidence to step forward."

~ **Cheryl Chumley**
*Online opinion editor, commentary writer & host of "Bold and Blunt" podcast at The Washington Times, and best-selling author of several non-fiction and fiction books*

"In *Spark Your Influence*, Misty Phillip dismantles the lie that leadership must come at the cost of peace and family. With wisdom and grace, she weaves biblical principles with practical steps to help women lead with confidence—free from fear, compromise, and burnout. If you're a woman of faith seeking to make a lasting impact for God's kingdom, this book is a must-read!"

~ **Dr. Trudy Simmons, Counselor/Coach/Host**

"Misty Phillip delivers a timely and inspiring call to Christian women to step into their influence with faith and purpose. *Spark Your Influence* is both encouraging and practical, providing the tools and wisdom needed to lead with excellence in any sphere. A must-read for women who want to make a lasting impact."

~ **Tracey Mitchell, HDD**
*Published Author/International Speaker*

"Misty Phillip isn't just a woman that offers a spark of truth and light, she's a woman that offers that spark while simultaneously fanning flames for others through her encouragement and innovative leadership. In her new book, *Spark Your Influence: Empowering Women to Lead with Boldness, Purpose, and Passion*, you'll discover why it's vital to lead as a Godly woman in this day and age and how to do so within the gifts, talents, and skills God has given you. Sometimes the only way to get a leadership spark to set a blaze is by breathing God's words of life over it. Are you allowing life-giving words to be received? Are you speaking them over yourself and others? As you read this book, may you also rise up to be resilient in focused servant leadership to influence those around you to do the same. It's time to stoke the flames of your influence."

**~ Wendie Pett, ND**

"When it comes to leadership, Misty Phillip lives what she teaches. With solid framework and strategies, she shares not only how to make an impact, but how to honor God while influencing others. A must read for anyone wanting a clear path to leadership and spiritual growth."

**~ Gari Meacham**
*Author of Spirit Hunger, Watershed Moments, and Truly Fed*
*Podcast co-host of the Gutsy Faith show*
*CEO of The Vine Uganda, a nonprofit organization in rural Africa.*

"Setting herself apart (not just with trademark hats), Misty Phillip knows that if you're going to cut through today's cluttered culture and influence others, it's essential to have an effective strategy. It starts with Biblical wisdom, but Misty equips you even further in "Spark Your Influence" by giving personal and actionable steps to propel your career and purpose and leave a lasting legacy."

~ Kathleen Cooke
*Co-founder of Cooke Media Group and The Influence Lab/Influence Women*

"What I love about Misty is that she's a go-getter—never afraid to step into new areas of influence to reach the culture for Jesus. She's bold, innovative, and always willing to try new things, and that same spirit fills the pages of *Spark Your Influence*. This book is a powerful guide for Christian women ready to embrace their leadership calling with confidence and faith. Misty offers both biblical wisdom and practical strategies to help women lead with purpose—without fear, burnout, or compromise. If you're looking for the encouragement and tools to step fully into your God-given influence, this book is for you!"

~ Krissy Miles
*Pastor | Business Strategist | Media Executive
Executive Director of The Nfluence Network,
Co-Founding Pastor Nfluence Church*

*Spark Your Influence* is another outstanding "don't miss this" Misty Phillip creation. This guide is filled with the wisdom, experience, and inspiration women need to become the leaders God has designed and called them to be. As always, Misty pours out her heart to the reader in such a genuine and relatable way that you cannot help but be moved to reach up, take God's hand, and follow Him to new heights of leadership.

~ **Lee Ann Mancini**
*CEO & Founder of Raising Christian Kids*
*Author of Raising Kids to Follow Christ,*
*Podcaster, Speaker, Adjunct Professor*
*Executive Producer & Author of the Sea Kids*
*Books & Animation Series*

Misty Phillip is an anointed voice calling us as women to wholeheartedly follow Christ into our next adventure. She inspires us to lead with conviction, marked by Spirit-led boldness and faith-filled courage. In Spark Your Influence she issues a clarion call to step into our identity as daughters of the Most High God, and from that secure position to overcome fear with creative expression that stirs us to embrace our purpose with passion. If you're ready to be encouraged, validated, and enthusiastically challenged, this book is just what you need for the next step in your life journey!

~ **Michelle Watson Canfield, PhD, LPC**
*Author, Let's Talk: Conversation Starters for*
*Dads and Daughters*
*Podcast host, The Dad Whisperer*

# SPARK YOUR INFLUENCE

Inspiring Women to Lead with
Boldness, Purpose, and Passion

**Spark Your Influence:**
*Inspiring Women to Lead with Boldness, Purpose, and Passion*

Copyright © 2025 by Misty Phillip

Published in association with Boss Media
https://michellerobinsonmedia.com

All rights reserved. No part of this publication may be reproduced, stored in a retrieval system, or transmitted in any form or by any means—electronic, mechanical, photocopy, recording or any other—except for brief quotations in printed reviews without the written prior permission of the publisher.

The website addresses recommended throughout this book are offered as a resource to you. These websites are not intended in any way to be or imply an endorsement on the part of Boss Media, nor do we vouch for their content.

No AI Training. Any use of this publication to "train" artificial intelligence (AI) technologies to generate text is expressly prohibited.

Unless otherwise noted, Scripture quotations are from the ESV® Bible (The Holy Bible, English Standard Version®), copyright © 2001 by Crossway, a publishing ministry of Good News Publishers. Used by permission. All rights reserved.

Book Cover by Peter Phillip
Edited by Criss Bertling
Print ISBN: 978-1-961074-19-4

# Dedication

Jesus, thank you for choosing to use me to impact the world. You truly do use the foolish things of the world to confound the wise. You are my joy and source of strength. You graciously saved me from destruction and granted me a life filled with beauty and adventure. I am eternally grateful.

I am especially thankful to my husband Peter for his relentless love and support in all my creative pursuits and crazy ideas. You are my rock! To my three wonderful, supportive sons, Jacob, Connor, and Ian, your love and encouragement inspire and empower me every day.

Thank you to all my friends for encouraging me to live a life filled with beauty, purpose, and intention, and for passing down a legacy of love, integrity, and resourcefulness.

Finally, many thanks to the Spark Media Community for rallying around my dream to change the world through podcasting. It has been my great honor to lead and serve you.

# Foreword

When I first met Misty, I was in the process of stepping out in obedience to God's calling—a calling to disrupt the movie industry for His glory, despite having no prior experience in film production I was determined with God's help to build a studio. It was at a conference that I had the privilege of meeting Misty Phillip, and I quickly realized how rare it is to come across a woman who not only lives with a spirit of excellence but also seeks to build others up in their God-given talents and callings. Misty is one of those individuals who embodies this principle in every aspect of her life.

It is a true honor to write the foreword for *Spark Your Influence: Inspiring Women to Lead with Boldness, Purpose, and Passion.* This book is not just a collection of leadership strategies or success tips; it is a powerful invitation to embrace the creativity, purpose, and passion God has uniquely entrusted to each of us. Misty's message encourages us to reject the traps of hustle and burnout, calling us to lead as Christian women who are grounded in faith, driven by purpose, and empowered to make an eternal impact.

As long as we hold a place of influence, we are called to lead. Leadership is not only about the results we achieve, but more importantly, about the lives we touch and the legacy we leave behind. In *Spark Your Influence,* Misty challenges us to trust God's direction in our lives, reassuring us that obedience to His call always leads to greater things.

What I love about Misty is her understanding of the balance required to lead boldly while serving others humbly. She brings her own experiences—her struggles, triumphs, and growth—into this book, offering us a real, honest blueprint for overcoming fear, building a solid foundation of faith, and creating a life of sustainable, impactful leadership.

Misty, thank you for your unwavering dedication to empowering women to lead with boldness and authenticity. This book has shown us it is truly amazing to be able to walk with courage, clarity, and confidence in the plans God has laid before us for our calling. As the owner of 4 the One Studio, I can personally attest to the impact of your friendship and encouragement in my own journey. This book is not just a guide; it is a catalyst for every woman ready to step into her divine calling and lead with purpose. I am proud to call you a friend, and I know that *Spark Your Influence* will help countless women become the leaders they were always meant to be.

With love and gratitude,

*Amber Butand*

**Owner, 4 the One Studio**

# Contents

Introduction .................................................................................................. 17

*Chapter 1*
**Embracing Your Creativity And Purpose**................................................ 21

*Chapter 2*
**God's Call For Women To Steward And Redeem Their Time** ........................ 37

*Chapter 3*
**God's Design For Women Leaders** ................................................................ 49

*Chapter 4*
**Answering God's Call To Lead With Courage And Conviction** ..................... 63

*Chapter 5*
**Navigating Respect And Authority**................................................................79

*Chapter 6*
**The Myth Of The "Hustle" And Reclaiming A God-Centered, Creative Life** ................................................................................................. 93

*Chapter 7*
**Creating Boundaries And Avoiding Burnout**.........................................109

*Chapter 8*
**Overcoming Fear And Embracing Courage**...........................................127

*Chapter 9*
**Discerning God's Voice**.............................................................................151

*Chapter 10*
**Building A Foundation Of Faith** ................................................................. 165

*Chapter 11*
**Aligning Vision And Strategy With God's Purpose** ........................................... 177

*Chapter 12*
**Servant Leadership And Putting Others First** ................................................. 193

*Chapter 13*
**Innovation For Leaders And Entrepreneurs** ................................................... 207

*Chapter 14*
**Building A Supportive Community** ................................................................ 219

*Chapter 15*
**Embracing God's Direction In Seasons Of Transition** ..................................... 235

*Chapter 16*
**Navigating Seasons Of Growth And Change** ................................................. 251

*Chapter 17*
**Finishing Strong And Leaving A Legacy** ........................................................ 267

*Chapter 18*
**Answering The Call** .................................................................................... 283

**Final Thoughts** .......................................................................................... 299

**Appendix Resources** .................................................................................. 305

**Assessments** ............................................................................................. 309

# Introduction

Hello, Sweet Friends

We live in a time like no other—when God is calling and empowering His daughters to rise up, lead, and accomplish extraordinary work. The world is shifting. We are at a pivotal moment in history where women's voices are not only needed but are divinely appointed to inspire, encourage, and generate change. Y'all, this is our moment! It is our opportunity to boldly step into everything God has prepared for us, not out of ambition but out of obedience to His call. I'm not talking about some feminist movement, but a move of women wholly submitted to God and the call He has on our lives.

We are uniquely positioned to lead with grace, wisdom, and strength that come not from ourselves and vain ambition but from our humble surrender and deep, abiding faith in God. The challenges we face are significant, but the God we serve is so much more! In every corner of society—from our homes and workplaces to our communities—there is a desperate need for leadership grounded in truth, compassion, love, humility, and unwavering faith.

Every single one of us leaves fingerprints on the world, whether we realize it or not. That sweater you gave your sister? She wears it whenever she needs a boost of courage. The playlist you made for your friend? It got her through some really dark days. That book recommendation you casually mentioned? Someone stayed up all night reading it, and it changed their entire perspective. It's wild how the smallest things we do ripple out in ways we rarely get to see. Like when you told someone they did a great job, and they went home walking a little taller. Or how your old college roommate still makes that recipe you taught them, and now their kids love it too.

We are all threads in God's big tapestry. Every kind word, every thoughtful gesture, every moment of showing up for someone, it matters. It really matters. Never think you're not making a difference in this world. Your impact is like those seeds that scatter in the wind. You may never see where they all land, but, girl, they're growing something beautiful somewhere. We may never understand the magnitude of our influence, but trust me, God and people are always watching.

In *Spark Your Influence*, we will explore what it means to lead as a woman of God in these critical times. We will discover how to harness the gifts and talents the Lord has placed within us to build His kingdom here on earth and to fulfill our God-given assignments. This is not just about filling positions or climbing ladders; it's about embracing the divine purpose for which we were uniquely created. It's about stepping into the fullness of who we are in Christ and leading others with the love, courage, and conviction that only He can provide.

The time is now. It is TIME to STAND UP and *SPARK YOUR INFLUENCE!* God is calling you to be a leader, not merely a follower. This is your moment to shine for His glory, to make a difference in the lives of those around you, and to leave a legacy of faith. Let's answer that call together.

This book is a declaration of intent—a call to action for every woman who feels God's tug on her heart to lead. My aim is to equip and inspire you to step confidently and firmly into your calling and leadership role. Throughout these pages, you will find biblical principles. All Scriptures are provided in the ESV translation. You will encounter practical advice and personal stories from my life and entrepreneurial journey, intended to encourage and assist you in navigating your own leadership path.

When I first stepped into leadership, I was genuinely terrified—like butterflies-in-my-stomach, waking-up-in-the-middle-of-the-night terrified! I'd lie in bed asking myself, "Who am I to do this?" Girl, let me tell you, those doubt monsters were having a field day in my mind! It was tough, y'all. Really tough. There were many days when I wanted to throw in the towel and run back to my comfort zone.

But do you know what? That's exactly where God does His best work—right in the middle of our mess and uncertainty. He was molding me through all those sleepless nights and wobbly moments even though I couldn't see it.

There have been many challenges to overcome along the way: fear, doubt, warfare, and even failure. But each obstacle offered an opportunity to grow, learn, and depend more fully on God. Embracing my leadership potential meant letting go of my insecurities and stepping boldly into the role God had prepared for me. As I did, I discovered a more profound sense of purpose and fulfillment than I ever imagined possible.

It is my prayer that this book empowers you to embrace your God-given potential to lead with the authority that comes from knowing who you are in Christ, be it in your home, the marketplace, your community, or ministry. Leadership is not about positions or titles;

it is about growth, influence, impact, and making a difference in the lives of others.

Dear friend, do not shrink back. God has uniquely crafted you for a purpose. It is time for you to walk boldly in your calling with purpose and passion. Together, let's step wholeheartedly into all the places and spaces God has prepared for us to make a lasting impact on His kingdom.

> *"Now to him who is able to do far more abundantly than all that we ask or think, according to the power at work within us, to him be glory in the church and in Christ Jesus throughout all generations, forever and ever. Amen."*
>
> ~ Ephesians 3:20-21

With Much Love & By His Grace,

*Misty Phillip*

# Embracing Your Creativity And Purpose

Within each of us dwells a spark. Our Creator places this spark in us to help us fulfill His unique purpose for our lives and to ignite others along the way. We each possess a distinct combination of gifts, talents, creativity, personality, skills, and life experiences intentionally and uniquely crafted by God to help us fulfill His purposes and assignments in our lives. When we embrace our God-given spark, we are transformed in how we lead, influence, and impact the world for His glory.

> *When we embrace our God-given spark, we are transformed in how we lead, influence, and impact the world for His glory.*

Friends, now is the time to fully step into all God that has for you as a leader so you can influence and impact others with boldness, purpose, and passion. I want you to live and lead an extraordinary life with the courage, commitment, and confidence that comes from knowing who God created you to be so you can do amazing things in partnership with Him and for His glory!

## Scriptural Foundation

*"So God created man in his own image, in the image of God he created him; male and female he created them."*

**~ Genesis 1:27**

*"For we are God's handiwork, created in Christ Jesus to do good works, which God prepared in advance for us to do."*

**~ Ephesians 2:10**

*"Do you not know that in a race all the runners run, but only one receives the prize? So run that you may obtain it. Every athlete exercises self-control in all things. They do it to receive a perishable wreath, but we are imperishable. So I do not run aimlessly; I do not box as one beating the air. But I discipline my body and keep it under control, lest after preaching to others I myself should be disqualified."*

**~ 1 Corinthians 9:24-27**

## A Spark and a Prayer

It all began with a simple prayer. "How do my gifting and calling align in the next season of my life, Lord?" It was a prayer whispered amidst a flow of tears in a moment of total vulnerability and transparency as I sat in my bathtub desperately seeking God's direction for the next season of my life. Never had I imagined that He would choose me, with all my flaws and failings, to inspire and lead others. Yet during that intimate moment with the Lord, tears streaming down my face, God nudged my spirit with a new and unanticipated calling.

As I prayed and reflected on the life experiences that had shaped my life's journey—writing, blogging, podcasting, and the challenges I walked through as a wife, mother, sister, and friend—I came to realize that God had been preparing me all along for this new journey and adventure.

I saw podcasting as a unique opportunity to reach people around the globe in a more intimate and accessible way. As I explored the podcasting landscape, I noticed a gap—and a problem—I could solve in the marketplace. Few resources or communities were dedicated to the growth of Christian podcasters.

This realization sparked the idea for something bigger: a platform that would empower Christian communicators to share their messages with the world. The vision to start a Christian podcast conference was born from my simple prayer. It was not about launching an event but about creating a space for Christian voices to be heard, where people could connect and gather, allowing creativity and faith to intersect to glorify God.

The journey hasn't been easy; it has often been quite challenging. I have faced numerous moments of fear and uncertainty. I considered giving up, quitting. But God gently reminded me that He didn't expect me to do this alone or rely solely on my own strength; He was the one guiding and leading me. God opened doors and made connections. His anointing and blessing were evident everywhere. He never called me to perfection; He simply called me to trust Him, step out in faith, embrace the journey, and recognize that He was with me every step of the way.

With the Lord's help and that of family and friends, I launched the first Spark Christian Podcast Conference in February 2020. The rest, as they say, "is history." The Lord led me every step of the way. I sat with Him and my journal daily, seeking His wisdom on what He would have me do. Every phone call and email led to new connections with old school podcasters, hosting companies, and Christian pioneers. Through Spark, God united hundreds of people to encourage and inspire one another just weeks before a global pandemic.

My goal with Spark was always to create a community to equip, encourage, and empower Christian podcasters to create content that glorifies God and impacts the lives of others. The Spark conference quickly grew into a vibrant community, offering unique resources such as the Spark Collective and the Spark Media magazine (featuring highlights from the community while providing training and a supportive network for Christian podcasters at all experience levels).

My vision for Spark Media expanded beyond podcasting to create a movement bringing together Christian creators from multiple media types: writers, speakers, podcasters, filmmakers, and digital content creators. Spark Media became a hub for creative collaboration, a place where everyone, regardless of their form of media, could come together and learn from one another. Through the creation of conferences, workshops, retreats, and online communities, we were all rooted together in advancing the Kingdom of God through media.

The success of Spark Media today is a testament that God can use anyone to spread His message far and wide. Under my stewardship, Spark Media helped countless Christian communicators find their voices, grow their platforms, and impact the world in a meaningful way. Creating the Spark Media awards empowered podcasters to gain recognition, open doors for speaking engagements, receive book contracts, and receive funding for their non-profits. One podcaster received tens of thousands of dollars for theirs after receiving a Spark Media award. How cool is that!

As you will see, my story is one of faith, obedience, grit, perseverance, and a commitment to using my gifts and talents as a force for good in the world. If God can use me, He can use you for purposes beyond your wildest dreams.

## Embrace Your Spark

Creativity is part of the divine spark within us, a reflection of God's image. As women, we balance multiple roles: mother, wife, daughter, professional, and friend. But within each of us lies a unique creative potential that God has embedded there for a greater purpose. This creativity is not merely a hobby or a pastime; it is a calling, a means by which we can lead, influence, and impact the world around us.

Creativity is important to God because it reflects His very nature. In the beginning, God created the universe. His creativity is evident throughout the Bible and the magnificent world He created. Being made in His image, we, too, are called to be creative, to use our gifts to fulfill His purposes, and to glorify Him. When our creative spark is combined with leadership, creativity becomes a powerful force for good, allowing us to do amazing things such as craft a business, build a brand, start a non-profit, write a book, or start a ministry that honors God and inspires others.

> *Creativity is important to God because it reflects His very nature.*

## Creativity as a Reflection of the Creator

Your creativity is a calling from God to create, lead, and inspire others. The Bible tells us that we are made in the image of God (Genesis 1:27), and one of the most profound ways we reflect His image is through our ability to create. Just as God spoke the world into existence with creativity and purpose, we, too, are able to create, shape, and influence the world around us. We participate in the divine act of creation through art, writing, media, design, business, music, cooking, sewing, or any other form of creative expression. God has equipped you with the creativity and courage to step forward and lead.

Ephesians 2:10 reminds us that our creative abilities are intentional gifts from God, designed for a specific purpose. When we embrace these gifts, we step into the roles God has ordained for us, leading with confidence and grace.

That same Scripture reminds us, *"For we are God's handiwork, created in Christ Jesus to do good works, which God prepared in advance for us to do."* This verse emphasizes that our creative abilities are not accidental or insignificant; they are intentional gifts from God designed for a specific purpose. When we embrace these gifts, we can step into the roles God has ordained for us from before the foundation of the universe to lead with confidence and grace.

## The Call to Authenticity

In my late twenties or early thirties, I attended a ladies Bible study at my church. I was asked to lead the small breakout room with women who were giants in the faith at my church. Shaking in my boots, I reluctantly agreed. God used this baby step in my leadership journey to stretch, grow, and prepare me to take action.

Our ability to guide, inspire, and shape conversations becomes increasingly vital as we grow in influence. But how do we move beyond the boundaries that have previously defined us? How do we step into a larger space with confidence and authenticity?

Our journey begins by recognizing and embracing our unique voice. Psalm 139:14 reminds us that we are *"fearfully and wonderfully made."* Every facet of who you are—your strengths, perspectives, and even quirks—is intentional and purposeful in God's grand design.

When you lead authentically, you connect with others on a deeper level. You inspire trust and create a space where those around you feel seen and valued. Isn't that what people are craving? Don't we all need to feel seen and heard and find a space where we can feel safe to connect and collaborate?

> *When you lead authentically, you connect with others on a deeper level.*

Leading from a place of authenticity means fulfilling a calling, not just filling a role. It allows you to impact and influence everyone in your community and sphere of influence because it makes you relatable. Now more than ever, the world needs the exceptional, authentic you that God created you to be! Let's walk in our purpose and passion to brightly shine and show up in our uniqueness and authenticity so we can "spark" those around us.

## Discovering Your Divine Purpose

Did you know that each of us has a unique divine purpose? This purpose is not a destination but a journey of faith, obedience, and trust in God's good plan. Your purpose is intertwined with your gifts and calling. Recognizing these can lead to a life of fulfillment and impact.

Reflecting on our personal experiences helps us see how God has guided us all along. Your purpose is revealed through your passions, the things that move you, and the natural talents God has blessed you with. Your divine purpose is not a destination but a journey of faith, obedience, and trust in God's good plan. We must be patient and trust that our faith and God's providence will guide us down the right path with all its twists and turns to our divine destiny. Every single one of us has a purpose in life. Yes, discovering exactly what that is can be challenging. But we can gain clues to our purpose through prayer and seeking wise counsel from trusted advisors who will help us process and find clarity in moments of uncertainty.

Have you ever wondered why you are here? What is the purpose of your life? Discovering your gifting, assignment, and calling can be a great place to start if you are seeking answers to these questions.

Here are some additional questions to get your creative juices flowing:

- ✦ What are you passionate about?
- ✦ What makes you angry?
- ✦ Are you naturally drawn to help a specific group (widows, orphans, singles, children, married couples)?
- ✦ What is your "zone of genius"?

I believe we all have a "zone of genius" where our gifts, talents, hard work, and creativity come together in a beautiful display of God's handiwork. When we explore these questions, spend time in prayer, seek wise counsel, and remain patient, God will unfold His plans for our lives.

Girl, you were created on purpose for a purpose! The really cool thing is God has specific work for each of us to do— work He prepared before the beginning of time. Understanding that God has a unique purpose for each of us can be both exhilarating yet sometimes feel a little overwhelming. Rest assured, my friend, no one else can do the work God has prepared for you. He has uniquely gifted you for the specific tasks ahead. He is the One who will open doors and guide your steps.

## Co-Creators and Co-Laborers

We are not merely creatives but co-laborers with God in His grand design. We are called to love God and love people with our hearts, souls, minds, and strength.

> *'And you shall love the Lord your God with all your heart and with all your soul and with all your mind and with all your strength.' The second is this: 'You shall love your neighbor as yourself.' There is no other commandment greater than these.*
>
> ~ Mark 12:30-31

We have the incredible opportunity to be used by God to love others and fulfill His Kingdom's purposes. Friends, your voice matters, and your gifts are needed because the world needs your unique creative spark!

Our creativity is not an isolated gift but a powerful tool we can wield in partnership with God. As co-laborers, our mission extends beyond the art we create or the businesses we build. It's about loving God and loving people while using our gifts and talents for the benefit of others.

We get to co-labor with the God of the universe. Our divine partnership with Him empowers us to pour our heart, soul, mind, and strength into everything we do. When we embrace our creativity and calling, our lives become a conduit through which God's love flows, where we can touch lives, influence others, and transform our communities. We are called to create with purpose, lead with passion, and serve with humility, knowing that in all we do, we are co-creating with the Creator Himself.

## Stepping into Your Calling

*Each of us is on assignment from Him—chosen, appointed, and empowered to collaborate with Him to fulfill His will on earth.*

Scripture teaches us to do all for the glory of God—we are all called to glorify God in everything we do. Whether through loving and serving others, using our talents for the greater good, or fulfilling a specific calling, we each are responsible for answering the call on our lives with excellence.

When feelings of inadequacy arise, remember that God does not call the equipped; He equips the called. There is favor and a special anointing on your life for the works God has planned for you. Each of us is on assignment from Him—chosen, appointed, and empowered to collaborate with Him to fulfill His will on earth.

God has given each of us a unique calling, something only we can do. It's far too easy to compare ourselves to others and feel like we're not enough. But God created each of us with a specific purpose in mind. Embrace who you are and what God has called you to do. The world needs what you have to offer, so step into your calling with boldness and confidence, trusting He will guide and lead you every step of the way.

## We are on Assignment

In 1 Corinthians, Paul reminds us that we are on assignment from God as believers. We are not here by accident but are chosen, appointed, and empowered by God to fulfill His will on earth. He reminds us that our lives are like a race. We must run with perseverance, intention, and discipline. Every step must be aligned with God's will, and every decision should reflect His love and truth in our lives.

> *We are not here by accident but are chosen, appointed, and empowered by God to fulfill His will on earth.*

I don't run much anymore, but when I was younger, I loved to run! When you are in a race, you must keep your eyes focused on the finish line. There will be times when you want to quit or give up, yet it in those moments that you must dig deep for resilience and keep your eyes fixed on Him.

> *Do you not know that in a race all the runners run, but only one receives the prize? So run that you may obtain it. Every athlete exercises self-control in all things. They do it to receive a perishable wreath, but we are imperishable. So I do not run aimlessly; I do not box as one beating the air. But I discipline my body and keep it under control, lest after preaching to others I myself should be disqualified.*
>
> ~ 1 Corinthians 9:24-27.

Paul emphasizes that our lives are like races, which we are to run with intention, discipline, and a focus on the ultimate prize: Jesus. The prize Paul refers to is not a temporary earthly reward but an eternal crown of righteousness.

My niece is a gifted cross-country and track runner. She is super disciplined. Each morning at the crack of dawn, she does her run or goes to practice. She maintains a healthy diet and follows a strict regime to prepare for her race. Her single goal is fixed in her mind: to win the prize. We too must be intentional in our spiritual race, keeping our eyes fixed on the prize, Jesus. Every step we take and every move we make should be aligned with God's will. Each decision we make should reflect His love and truth.

When we live on assignment from God, everything we do—our work, relationships, and daily choices— isn't just a series of mundane tasks. We have the opportunity every single day to surrender our will to His. Perhaps it's just shift in mindset from simply going through the motions or doing things our way to living an intentional lifestyle with passion and purpose. God has entrusted us with His message, His love, and His power to impact the world around us. I don't know about you, but there is no place I'd rather be than smack dab in the middle of God's will for my life.

Paul's words challenge us to consider: Are we running this race with perseverance with our eyes fixed on Jesus? Are we living out our assignment with passion?

Remember, we are on a mission from God; He has equipped us with everything we need to fulfill it. We must run our race with faith, knowing that our efforts are not in vain but are part of a more excellent, eternal plan.

## Application Questions

---

Reflecting on the idea that creativity is not just a hobby but a calling from God, how does this perspective change the way you view your creative gifts?

..................................................................................................

..................................................................................................

..................................................................................................

What steps can you take to align your creativity with God's purpose for your life?

..................................................................................................

..................................................................................................

..................................................................................................

What natural talents or gifts do you believe God has given you?

..................................................................................................

..................................................................................................

..................................................................................................

How have you used these gifts to serve others and fulfill your purpose?

..................................................................................................

..................................................................................................

..................................................................................................

How can you use your creative talents to glorify God and influence others?

..................................................................................................

..................................................................................................

..................................................................................................

# PRAYER

Sweet Jesus,

Help us embrace the creative spark you have placed within us to lead. Give us divine strategies to live authentically on assignment and in alignment with all you've called us to do and be. Give us wisdom and the courage to pursue our callings with boldness, passion, and purpose.

All for Your name's sake and YOUR glory! Amen.

# Notes

# God's Call For Women To Steward And Redeem Their Time

Time feels like a fleeting commodity. None of us knows how much time we have, yet we all receive the same 24 hours each day. People say the older you get, the faster time flies, and isn't that the truth? We are living in accelerated days. It could be because, as women, our days are busy with endless responsibilities, various distractions, and many demands pulling us in different directions that often divert us from our true purpose. Yet, as women called to live out God's plan, we are reminded that time is not ours to waste. It is a precious gift entrusted to us by our Creator to steward wisely.

I love the phrase "redeeming the time" in the Bible, probably because I love living with intentionality. This lifestyle is about aligning our hearts, minds, and actions with God's purpose for our lives. Every moment and every day offer ample opportunities to choose how we

> *God calls each of us to rise above the noise and distractions of life and to prioritize what truly matters most— our relationship with Him, our families, and the unique calling He has placed on each of our lives.*

live. Will we choose to glorify Him, serve others, and grow in faith, or will we squander our time on trivial, meaningless pursuits? God calls each of us to rise above the noise and distractions of life and to prioritize what truly matters most—our relationship with Him, our families, and the unique calling He has placed on each of our lives.

Let's examine how we can steward our time wisely and balance life's demands with grace. Let us strive to be women who walk boldly in faith, inspire others, and trust every season and every moment can be used for God's glory.

## Scriptural Foundation

*"An excellent wife who can find? She is far more precious than jewels. The heart of her husband trusts in her, and he will have no lack of gain. She does him good, and not harm, all the days of her life. She seeks wool and flax and works with willing hands. She is like the ships of the merchant; she brings her food from afar. She rises while it is yet night and provides food for her household and portions for her maidens. She considers a field and buys it; with the fruit of her hands, she plants a vineyard. She dresses herself with strength and makes her arms strong. She perceives that her merchandise is profitable.*

*"Her lamp does not go out at night. She puts her hands to the distaff, and her hands hold the spindle. She opens her hand to the poor and reaches out her hands to the needy. She is not afraid of snow for her household, for all her household are clothed in scarlet. She makes bed coverings for herself; her clothing is fine linen and purple. Her husband is known in the gates when he sits among the elders of the land. She makes linen garments and sells them; she delivers sashes to*

*the merchant. Strength and dignity are her clothing, and she laughs at the time to come. She opens her mouth with wisdom, and the teaching of kindness is on her tongue. She looks well to the ways of her household and does not eat the bread of idleness.*

*"Her children rise up and call her blessed; her husband also, and he praises her: 'Many women have done excellently, but you surpass them all.' Charm is deceitful, and beauty is vain, but a woman who fears the Lord is to be praised. Give her of the fruit of her hands, and let her works praise her in the gates."*

~ **Proverbs 31:10-31**

*"For it will be like a man going on a journey, who called his servants and entrusted to them his property. To one he gave five talents, to another two, to another one, to each according to his ability. Then he went away. He who had received the five talents went at once and traded with them, and he made five talents more. So also he who had the two talents made two talents more. But he who had received the one talent went and dug in the ground and hid his master's money.*

*"Now after a long time the master of those servants came and settled accounts with them. And he who had received the five talents came forward, bringing five talents more, saying, 'Master, you delivered to me five talents; here, I have made five talents more.' His master said to him, 'Well done, good and faithful servant. You have been faithful over a little; I will set you over much. Enter into the joy of your master.' And he also who had the two talents came forward, saying, 'Master, you delivered to me two talents; here, I have made two talents*

*more.' His master said to him, 'Well done, good and faithful servant. You have been faithful over a little; I will set you over much. Enter into the joy of your master.'*

*"He also who had received the one talent came forward, saying, 'Master, I knew you to be a hard man, reaping where you did not sow, and gathering where you scattered no seed, so I was afraid, and I went and hid your talent in the ground. Here, you have what is yours.' But his master answered him, 'You wicked and slothful servant! You knew that I reap where I have not sown and gather where I scattered no seed? Then you ought to have invested my money with the bankers, and at my coming, I should have received what was my own with interest. So take the talent from him and give it to him who has the ten talents. For to everyone who has will more be given, and he will have an abundance. But from the one who has not, even what he has will be taken away. And cast the worthless servant into the outer darkness. In that place, there will be weeping and gnashing of teeth."*

~ Matthew 25:14-30

## The Woman Who Fears the Lord

As women who desire to serve the Lord, our service begins with the posture of our hearts and how we intentionally live our lives. Proverbs 31:10-31 gives us a glimpse into the life of a woman who embodies both creativity and leadership. Yet she often gets a bad rap as a woman whose lifestyle is unattainable, a figure so perfect she seems out of reach for the modern woman.

Upon closer examination, we no longer just see a detailed checklist of duties and responsibilities but the beautiful portrait of a woman who embodies strength, wisdom, and creativity. The Proverbs 31 woman is a leader in her home and community, someone who is generous, diligent, and beautifully lives out her faith with purpose and intention. She exemplifies what it means to lead with integrity, love, and a deep reverence for God. All while caring for her home, family, and business. Her creativity is not separate from her leadership; it is the very foundation of it.

The Proverbs 31 woman fears the Lord; everything she does flows from her love for Him. Proverbs 9:10 tells us, *"The fear of the Lord is the beginning of wisdom, and the knowledge of the Holy One is insight."* This woman is a virtuous, wise, and strong leader who serves the Lord and others with excellence. Her story is a vibrant model for every woman who desires to step into her God-given role as a leader today.

## The Modern Proverbs 31 Woman

The modern Proverbs 31 woman uniquely blends this timeless wisdom and contemporary strength. She embodies the virtues laid out in Scripture but does so in a constantly changing world. She's not merely a homemaker, though she may excel in caring for her family. She's also a businesswoman, wise leader, creative, and a servant of God. The modern Proverbs 31 woman reflects God's grace and power in every aspect of her life. She understands that her worth is far above rubies, not because of what she does, but because of who she is in Christ. Her example is as relevant and inspiring today as it was in ancient times!

Today's Proverbs 31 woman wears many hats. If you know me, you know I love a good hat! She is a mom who nurtures her children with love and wisdom, and she guides them in the ways of the Lord. She is also a businesswoman and entrepreneur who runs her business with integrity. Always mindful that her success reflects God's blessing in her life. She uses her creative gifts to provide for her family and glorify God. Yet she is a supportive wife who stands by her husband's side as a partner and confidante, building a household and life that honors God. As women, we must not underestimate how important it is to be a helper to our husbands.

What I love the most about the modern P31 woman is that she is rooted and grounded in her faith, knowing her worth, identity, and strength all come from the Lord. She seeks His wisdom and draws on His wisdom in every decision she makes. Taking her needs to the Lord in prayer, she rises early to seek Him and lays down her head at night with a heart full of gratitude. Understanding her beauty is not only in her outward appearance, but in the kindness, generosity, and wisdom flowing through her relationship with God. The modern Proverbs 31 woman is a woman of valor who laughs without fear of the future because she knows God safely holds her in the palm of His hand, and she trusts in Him.

As a modern P31 woman, I've worked to be an example of diligence and influence, not striving to meet the world's expectations but instead seeking to fulfill God's purpose. It has looked different through my life's many ages and stages, from walking away from my career to homeschooling my kids or stepping out into multiple new careers in my mid-life. I've had to let go of some really good things in my life to make room for God's best. Recently, He has shown me that knowing when to quit something that isn't serving me or my family well is just as important as knowing when to start something new. Transitions can be tricky to navigate, but with His guidance, we can boldly step into all He has for us.

## Stewardship & Redeeming Your Time

As you step into your divine purpose, remember that time is a precious gift from God. The older I get, the more I realize I want to steward my remaining time on earth well. Ephesians 5:16 urges us to *"make the best use of the time, because the days are evil."* Every moment is a treasured gift and an opportunity to align our actions with His will and to use our gifts for His glory.

> *As you step into your divine purpose, remember that time is a precious gift from God.*

The "Parable of the Talents" we read about in Matthew 25:14-30 teaches us the importance of stewardship and God's expectations for His followers. We are stewards of the time and talents God has given us. He calls us to use them wisely for His glory.

In that parable, a man going on a journey calls three of his servants and entrusts them with his wealth in the form of talents—a unit of money. To the first servant, he gives five talents; to the second, two; and to the third, one talent. Each according to his ability. The man then departs on his journey. The first servant wisely invests his five talents, doubling his money. The second servant does the same with his two talents, also doubling his money. However, the third servant takes a different approach. Fearing the master's wrath and wanting to avoid any risk, he buries his single talent in the ground.

Upon his return, the master settles accounts with his servants. The first two servants present their doubled money and receive commendation and greater responsibilities from the master. They hear the words: *"Well done, good and faithful servant. You have been faithful over a little; I will set you over much. Enter into the joy of your master."* The third servant, however, explains that he hid the money to keep it safe and returns only the original talent. His master rebukes him, calling him wicked and lazy. He takes away his talent and gives it to the servant with ten talents.

> *If you want to be a leader, you must grasp the concept of stewardship.*

This story embodies several vital lessons we can apply to our lives, emphasizing the importance of stewardship. I once heard the expression: If you want to be a leader, you must grasp the concept of stewardship. You see, God entrusts each of us with gifts, talents, and resources, and He expects us to use them wisely. Stewardship also champions the idea of faithfulness. When we are faithful in small matters, it paves the way for greater responsibilities. It also serves as a reminder of the severe consequences of inaction, laziness, and fear, especially when one has been given much.

We each have the same 24 hours every day and are stewards of the time God has given us. He calls us to use it wisely for His glory. The Parable of the Talents is a compelling lesson about using what God has given us wisely and effectively. As you pursue your purpose, prioritize what truly matters: your relationship with God, caring for your family, fulfilling your calling, and loving others.

Every day is brimming with opportunities to glorify Him and serve others. I love traveling with my husband because my days are unencumbered with my usual work duties and household chores, which frees me up to be on a mission for Him. God will often put me in unexpected rooms and places where I can shine His light and share His love for others in fun and surprising ways. I call this being on an adventure with Jesus. And guess what? We can live our entire lives on an adventure with Jesus when we surrender our days to Him.

## Stewarding Your Gifts & Talents

We are blessed with unique gifts and talents intricately woven into our being by the Creator. Each gift is a present we get to discover, unwrap, and share with the world. These gifts and talents aren't just for our benefit but are key tools in fulfilling our kingdom purpose. Recently, I could tell l was getting off course with my purpose because I had a stinky attitude and was thinking more about myself than I was thinking of others. My "stinking thinking" prompted me to analyze the way I was using my time, talents, and resources to make some significant changes. Aligning our natural abilities with our zone of genius and spiritual calling is amazing because it unlocks a powerful synergy to move mountains and light up the world around us!

As you contemplate all the ways to steward your gifts, talents, time, and resources, pray about the many ways you can show up in the world as your authentic self to use your gifts and talents for the betterment of the world and for God's glory. Ask the Lord to give you divine strategies to help you steward your time and talents wisely.

## APPLICATION QUESTIONS

Reflect on how you currently spend your time. Are there areas where you feel distractions, or demands pull you away from God's purpose for your life? What practical steps can you take this week to realign your priorities with His will?

..................................................................................................

..................................................................................................

..................................................................................................

..................................................................................................

..................................................................................................

The modern Proverbs 31 woman balances faith, family, and her calling with grace and intentionality. How can you better steward your gifts and talents in this season of your life? How can you ensure your creativity and leadership align with God's glory?

..................................................................................................

..................................................................................................

..................................................................................................

..................................................................................................

..................................................................................................

The Parable of the Talents emphasizes the importance of using what God has entrusted to us. How can you effectively steward your time and talents to serve others and advance God's Kingdom? How might fear or hesitation hold you back, and how can you overcome it?

.................................................................................................................

.................................................................................................................

.................................................................................................................

.................................................................................................................

# PRAYER

*Heavenly Father,*

*God of the Universe and Creator of all things, thank You for the unique gifts and talents You have placed within us. Help us discover and embrace these gifts with boldness, recognizing that our spark is not just for our enjoyment but for Your glory and the advancement of Your Kingdom. Lead and guide us as we step into the leadership roles You have prepared for us so we can use our talents and creative abilities to influence and inspire others. May we always seek Your wisdom first as we co-labor with You to craft a life and a legacy that honors You.*

*In Jesus' name, we pray. Amen.*

# God's Design For Women Leaders

Have you ever considered how God has uniquely designed you as a leader? He has designed and created you with specific passions, gifts, and talents that will serve you and others on your leadership journey. All of these traits were intentionally woven into your being by the Creator Himself when He created you so you could accomplish all He has called you to do.

As women, we often find ourselves juggling while balancing many responsibilities. We sense there is more to this life than dishes, laundry, and carpool lines. We may even long to lead and impact those around us, in our homes, communities, or the marketplace. Yet, the world sends conflicting messages about what leadership should look like, leaving many of us questioning how to reconcile our faith with our calling and what it means to be a leader.

I recently consulted with a friend who struggles with mindset issues around making money and equating that to success. She is a multi-gifted and passionate leader but has struggled to find her footing since becoming an empty nester. Her mindset 'blocks' stem from the fact that both she and her husband have a background in finance and do not recognize that leadership isn't just about climbing ladders, breaking barriers, or chasing after societal definitions of success.

Authentic, God-ordained leadership begins with a heart surrendered to God.

When we place our dreams, ambitions, and callings into God's hands, He transforms them into something far greater than we could accomplish on our own. This is the essence of leadership rooted in faith—allowing God to guide our steps, shape our vision, and use our influence for His glory.

In this chapter, we will examine God's design for women leaders by exploring Scripture and biblical examples of women leaders like Deborah, Esther, and Lydia. We'll uncover how God has always called and equipped women to lead for His purposes. Together, we'll discover how to embrace our unique identity as women, step into our God-given roles boldly, and lead in a way that reflects His grace and strength.

*Leadership isn't about striving for perfection or proving your worth.*

As we dive into this topic, remember this: your identity as a leader is first and foremost rooted in being a daughter of the King. Leadership isn't about striving for perfection or proving your worth. It's about faithfully stewarding the gifts God has entrusted to you. Whether you lead a business, a family, or a ministry, God has uniquely equipped you to influence the world in a way only you can.

Let's embark on this journey together—embracing God's design, rejecting the world's pressures, and stepping into leadership with confidence, courage, and a heart committed to Him. You were made for this moment, and God is ready to establish your plans as you commit them to His purpose.

## Scriptural Foundation

*"Commit your work to the Lord, and your plans will be established."*

~ **Proverbs 16:3**

*«As each has received a gift, use it to serve one another, as good stewards of God's varied grace: whoever speaks, as one who speaks oracles of God; whoever serves, as one who serves by the strength that God supplies—in order that in everything God may be glorified through Jesus Christ. To him belong glory and dominion forever and ever. Amen.»*

~ **1 Peter 4:10-11**

*"There is neither Jew nor Greek, there is neither slave nor free, there is no male and female, for you are all one in Christ Jesus."*

~ **Galatians 3:28**

## The Glass Ceiling Paradox: Embracing a God-Centered Perspective for Women

When I started Spark Media, I had a friend who was enamored by what I'd done as a leader in the podcast space. She would always thank me for breaking the glass ceiling and paving the way for women in podcasting. In our modern culture, breaking the glass ceiling is a compelling metaphor for women achieving high-level positions of leadership and influence, particularly in fields historically dominated by men. While striving for professional equality is a worthwhile goal, it can promote a mindset that conflicts with a Christ-centered perspective.

The term "glass ceiling" implies that a woman's worth or significance hinges on her ability to climb the corporate ladder or achieve a particular societal status. Sometimes the quest to break the glass ceiling takes on an almost militant urgency, reducing one's worth to career achievements and perpetuating the idea that a woman must prove her value by outdoing her male counterparts. This way of thinking can further exacerbate the relentless "hustle culture," leading many women to feel perpetually inadequate unless they're smashing societal barriers and hustling their way to the top.

## We are Image-Bearers

First and foremost, our primary identity comes from being children of God, not from any professional milestones or societal expectations we may meet or exceed. The Apostle Paul makes this clear in Galatians 3:28, stating, *"There is neither Jew nor Greek, there is neither slave nor free, there is no male and female, for you are all one in Christ Jesus."* This verse encourages us to look beyond worldly status and see ourselves and others through the lens of divine equality as image-bearers. We are God's representatives on this earth and conduits of His love.

> *Our primary identity comes from being children of God*

It's worth noting that the Bible does not discourage ambition or the desire to lead. Many strong, influential women, such as Deborah, Esther, Lydia, and others, appear in the Scriptures. These women served God and their communities with courage and wisdom. However, their significance did not come solely from their roles or achievements but from their willingness to follow God's plan for their lives.

Striving to break the glass ceiling should not be an end but a means of serving God more effectively. We shouldn't chase after positions of power or prestige for our own sake but to equip ourselves to better fulfill the mission that God has set before us.

> *Striving to break the glass ceiling should not be an end but a means of serving God more effectively.*

## Women Leaders

Leadership is a calling God extends to many women. Throughout Scripture, we see powerful examples of women who embraced their God-given roles as leaders, shaping history and advancing God's Kingdom in remarkable ways. Understanding and stepping into this leadership role can feel overwhelming, especially in a world that often presents conflicting messages about what it means to lead or even what it means to be a woman.

My son's physical therapist once told me I was intense. I was shocked to hear him tell me that because I had always considered myself to be merely driven and excited. I've now come to accept that God has wired me to be intense too. God uses this intensity in my life to keep me focused and helps me blaze trails.

In this chapter, we'll delve into God's design for women leaders by looking at real-world examples. We'll explore how God has uniquely empowered women for leadership, the vision He has for them, and the profound impact we can have when fully embracing His calling. Through the lives of Deborah, Esther, and Lydia, we'll witness how women have historically stepped into leadership roles with courage, wisdom, and faith. This understanding will inspire and embolden us as we seek to lead in our creative fields today.

## Scriptural Foundation for Women Leaders

Let's begin by grounding our understanding in Scripture, which provides a clear vision of God's design for leadership. Two key verses—Proverbs 16:3 and 1 Peter 4:10-11—offer a blueprint for how women can approach leadership in a way that honors God and fulfills His purpose. Proverbs 16:3 tells us to, *"Commit your work to the Lord, and your plans will be established."* This verse speaks directly to the heart of leadership. Our plans, dreams, and ambitions should be submitted to God and His will for our lives. When we commit our lives to Him and give our leadership roles to the Lord, He is faithful to guide us, establish our steps, and bring our plans to fruition according to His will every step of the way. Leadership isn't about striving in our own strength to make everything happen but a continuous surrender of our work to Him, trusting He will lead us. *"Humble yourselves, therefore, under the mighty hand of God so at the proper time He may exalt you."* 1 Peter 5:6.

1 Peter 4:10-11 teaches us about the stewardship of our gifts.

> *As each has received a gift, use it to serve one another, as good stewards of God's varied grace: whoever speaks, as one who speaks oracles of God; whoever serves, as one who serves by the strength that God supplies—in order that in everything God may be glorified through Jesus Christ. To him belong glory and dominion forever and ever. Amen.*

This passage calls us to recognize that our leadership abilities are gifts from God, given to us not for our glory but to serve others and bring glory to Him. Leadership is a form of stewardship, a responsibility to use our influence, talents, and resources for the benefit of others and to further God's Kingdom.

## God is Using Women Mightily in the Last Days

I have a friend who says it was a woman who brought God into the world, and it will be women ushering him back. Have you noticed how God is raising armies of women and mightily using women's voices today? I had the privilege of attending the Million Praying Women's Vigil at the National Mall in Washington, DC, to pray for our children, families, and nation; to pray for repentance for our country and for God to heal our land. This movement is spearheaded by a fierce woman of God, Jenny Donnelly.

> *I have a friend who says it was a woman who brought God into the world, and it will be women ushering him back.*

God is calling mothers to plead the blood of Jesus over their families and to raise the next generation for Christ. He also uses women as business owners and non-profit leaders, para-church organizations, authors, speakers, podcasters, and Christian media to make a global impact on promoting truth and exposing the darkness. I love seeing women lock arms and march alongside their male counterparts to make a Kingdom impact. The role of women in God's plan is essential and significant, even though women have often been overlooked or unappreciated by their male counterparts within the church. We are seeing a resurgence of women who are not afraid to walk in the fullness of their calling to be obedient to God and make a difference in the world.

When I look at the many ways God uses women to fulfill His kingdom's purposes, I see that they are both inspiring and transformative. I love watching women rise up with boldness and courage to step into the roles and opportunities that were once deemed beyond their reach. I especially love watching women collaborate, celebrate each other, and create growth opportunities for one another. We can overcome the challenges we face and boldly walk in our divine purpose when we lock arms with our sisters. We are all raised up when we come together for a common purpose.

We can boldly pursue our goals and break through barriers, all while celebrating our God-given femininity by walking in the humility, grace, and strength that comes from the Lord. We can boldly proclaim the Good News and bring hope and healing to a hurting world—from the board room to the mission fields to the marketplace. Our voices echo the call of God, and our actions are having an eternal impact.

*Our voices echo the call of God, and our actions are having an eternal impact.*

One of the most profound ways God uses women is in leadership within the church and ministry. We are teaching, mentoring, and leading in congregations, organizing community outreaches, and spearheading movements outside of the four walls of the church building to reach the world. For many years and in many denominations, women's voices have been silenced in the church, but God is making a way for women to stand up and have their voices be heard. These women, filled with the Holy Spirit, are igniting passion and purpose in others, demonstrating that leadership is not confined to gender but is a matter of calling and anointing. Their influence molds the next generation of believers and equips them to stand firm in their faith and live boldly for Christ.

## God is using Women at Home, in the Marketplace & Ministry

In the family unit, women are the heart and soul of the home and family, and have the incredible opportunity to nurture both the spiritual and physical well-being of those under their care. Godly mothers and grandmothers instill biblical values and principles into their children and grandchildren, creating a legacy of faith that transcends generations. These women are prayer warriors who stand in the gap for their families, and their prayers are ushering in breakthroughs and miracles. They reflect God's heart and exemplify His character's nurturing aspect through their love and sacrifice.

Women are also making significant strides in the marketplace, where their presence and influence are remarkable. These amazing women are bringing integrity, compassion, and a Christ-centered approach to business, transforming workplaces into environments where God's principles are upheld. As entrepreneurs, executives, and professionals, women are proving faith and work are not adversaries requiring us to pick a side, but that they can coexist harmoniously.

> *Women are also making significant strides in the marketplace, where their presence and influence are remarkable.*

One of my besties, Kelly Buckner, exemplifies these characteristics in her Bee Bold consulting practice as a Visual Brand Strategist and consultant. Through Bee Bold, she inspires individuals to embrace their unique gifts, live courageously, and make a lasting impact in their communities by teaching them skills to maximize their brand and business. Over the years, I watched Kelly successfully navigate the twists and turns of being a business owner, pivoting when necessary, and staying ahead of the curve to offer timely resources for her clients.

Another example is my beautiful friend, Amber Butaud, owner of the 4 The One Studio, a creative space dedicated to capturing authentic moments through photography and videography. Amber boldly stepped out to start a movie production studio, and to disrupt the movie industry for God's glory because God called her to it, even though she had no prior experience or background in the industry. With a passion for storytelling and a heart for serving others, Amber uses her gifts and talents to create meaningful content that inspires and uplifts.

These ladies approach their business with a spirit of excellence and Christlikeness. I've loved watching God use them to build others up in their giftings and callings. Their success stories are a testament to God's favor and blessing. Their impact extends beyond financial success, as they mentor and support others while fostering a culture of empowerment and collaboration.

Lastly, in mission fields around the world, women are fearlessly proclaiming the Gospel in places where the name of Jesus has never been heard. God is using each of these brave women to spread His love and truth, fulfill the Great Commission, and bring His kingdom closer with each passing day. They are serving in remote villages, urban slums, and war-torn regions, bringing the light of Christ to the darkest corners of the earth.

My sweet friend Gari Meacham founded The Vine Uganda and dedicated her efforts to empowering women, educating children, and providing care for vulnerable populations in Uganda. Gari's work includes initiatives that serve as a haven for abandoned infants, and partnerships with organizations to address critical needs like clean water access. Gari shares the love of Christ by fostering hope, transformation, and sustainable change in Ugandan communities. Her dedication and perseverance to saving lives and souls and her stories of sacrifice and service inspire countless others to follow in her footsteps.

Obedience isn't always easy, but it's always worth it. When God calls us to do something extraordinary, He always equips us with everything we need to accomplish it. Our job is to say yes and trust Him with the outcome. Walking in obedience is about surrendering our will to His and trusting His plan—which is always better than anything we could imagine. There are countless blessings tied to our obedience.

> *Obedience isn't always easy, but it's always worth it.*

## APPLICATION QUESTIONS

How does the understanding that our primary identity comes from being children of God, rather than professional achievements, impact the way you approach your leadership roles?

.................................................................................................

.................................................................................................

.................................................................................................

.................................................................................................

.................................................................................................

In what areas of your life do you feel the pressure to "break the glass ceiling," and how can you shift your focus to align more closely with a Christ-centered perspective?

.................................................................................................

.................................................................................................

.................................................................................................

.................................................................................................

.................................................................................................

How do you feel God is calling you to step into leadership, and what fears or challenges are holding you back from fully embracing this calling?

..................................................................................................

..................................................................................................

..................................................................................................

..................................................................................................

# PRAYER

*Heavenly Father,*

*Help us to boldly lead wherever you call us. Help us to glean the wisdom we need to lead from the examples we see in Scripture, and surround us with supportive women who encourage us higher. Help us to understand our true identities as daughters and image bearers so we can lead with courage and grace. Align our thoughts with yours and help us to live in radical obedience and abundance.*

*In Jesus name, we pray. Amen.*

# Answering God's Call To Lead With Courage And Conviction

Today, God is raising up modern-day Esthers and Deborahs— women who are boldly stepping into their God-ordained callings. These women are not defined by their circumstances or limited by the expectations of others. Instead, they are fueled by unwavering trust in God's promises, desiring to boldly step out in obedience to change the world.

The Esthers understand they have been placed in their positions "for such a time as this," and they are leveraging their influence to impact families, communities, and nations. Similarly, we see modern-day Deborahs as wise and fearless women who lead with wisdom, strength, and obedience to God's will. The Lydias are savvy businesswomen who open their hearts and homes to spread the gospel.

We see mothers shaping the next generation, entrepreneurs building businesses on kingdom principles, and leaders guiding others with discernment and grace. These women are answering God's call to be beacons of light and vessels of His truth in a world that so desperately needs both.

Throughout this chapter, we'll dive deeper into these biblical examples to see how their stories inspire us to lead courageously, serve generously, and fulfill God's unique purpose for our lives.

## Scriptural Foundation

*"For if you keep silent at this time, relief and deliverance will rise for the Jews from another place, but you and your father's house will perish. And who knows whether you have not come to the kingdom for such a time as this?"*

**~ Esther 4:14**

*"Now Deborah, a prophetess, the wife of Lappidoth, was judging Israel at that time. She used to sit under the palm of Deborah between Ramah and Bethel in the hill country of Ephraim, and the people of Israel came up to her for judgment."*

**~ Judges 4:4-5**

*"One who heard us was a woman named Lydia, from the city of Thyatira, a seller of purple goods, who was a worshiper of God. The Lord opened her heart to pay attention to what was said by Paul. And after she was baptized, and her household as well, she urged us, saying, 'If you have judged me to be faithful to the Lord, come to my house and stay.' And she prevailed upon us."*

**~ Acts 16:14-15**

Across the globe, women are stepping into positions of influence and leadership with the same courage and conviction displayed by biblical figures like Esther, Deborah, and Lydia—whether through business ventures, ministry work, creative pursuits, or community leadership.

## Deborah Led with Wisdom and Courage

Deborah, a prophetess instructed in divine knowledge, wife, and judge of Israel, used her wisdom and courage to lead her people. Among the heroes of ancient Israel, Deborah stands out as one of the most remarkable examples of a woman leader in Scripture. Her noble leadership bridged the sacred and secular worlds as both prophet and judge.

Her story unfolds in the book of Judges, where the enemy armies threatened her people. She didn't hesitate to rally the troops and march into battle when called upon. But what makes her story so fascinating isn't simply her military prowess. She served as the nation's highest authority, settling disputes under a palm tree and speaking with divine authority.

She never appears to doubt her calling or apologize for her power. She led guided by an unshakeable faith that God would deliver on His promises. At its heart, Deborah's narrative shows us something timeless about leadership—that it flows most naturally from a deep conviction about what's right and the courage to act on that conviction.

> *She never appears to doubt her calling or apologize for her power.*

## Esther Saved Her People from Destruction

Esther is another powerful example of female leadership, with her beauty, wisdom, and grace. The story of Esther reads like a political thriller in the Bible book of Esther. A young Jewish woman becomes queen of the world's most powerful empire through an unlikely series of events.

In a position of unique, significant influence as the queen of Persia, humility, wisdom, courage, and a deep sense of love and responsibility for her people marked her leadership. Esther's story highlights the importance of both timing and discernment in leadership. She understood the importance of fasting, praying, and when to boldly step forward. Esther could have quietly lived out her days in luxury, but when she learned of a plot to destroy her people, she was willing to risk everything. Esther sought God's guidance and decisively acted by approaching her husband-king to save her people.

*Esther's story highlights the importance of both timing and discernment in leadership.*

Esther's story isn't just about personal courage; it is a story of walking in humility and wisdom to navigate a potentially deadly crisis. Her story speaks to every woman who's ever wondered if they've been put in a position of influence for a bigger purpose than themselves. Esther's story reminds us that leadership often involves taking risks and making difficult decisions. When we seek God's guidance, He equips us with the strength and courage to stand up and fulfill our calling.

## Lydia Exercised Her Gifts in the Marketplace

Women's leadership roles in biblical times were remarkably diverse. Lydia led in the marketplace as an enterprising merchant and the first European convert to Christianity. To countless others serving both publicly and privately, these women shared an unshakeable faith and dedication to God's purpose.

Lydia's story unfolds in the New Testament book of Acts.

> *So, setting sail from Troas, we made a direct voyage to Samothrace, and the following day to Neapolis, and from there to Philippi, which is a leading city of the district of Macedonia and a Roman colony. We remained in this city some days. And on the Sabbath day we went outside the gate to the riverside, where we supposed there was a place of prayer, and we sat down and spoke to the women who had come together. One who heard us was a woman named Lydia, from the city of Thyatira, a seller of purple goods, who was a worshiper of God. The Lord opened her heart to pay attention to what was said by Paul. And after she was baptized, and her household as well, she urged us, saying, 'If you have judged me to be faithful to the Lord, come to my house and stay.' And she prevailed upon us.*
>
> ~ Acts 16:11-15.

In Acts 16:11-15, Lydia's leadership is evident in her hospitality and role in the early church. Lydia built a thriving business selling purple cloth and wasn't shy about using her success to help others. When

*What's fascinating about her story is how she bridged the worlds of commerce and faith.*

Paul and his companions needed support, she stepped up. What's fascinating about her story is how she bridged the worlds of commerce and faith. She didn't merely lead in church circles but brought her faith right into the marketplace. Her generosity and service showed what leadership could look like beyond traditional religious roles.

## Bold Faith to Walk in God's Strength Like the Women Leaders of Scripture

These women in the Bible didn't let anything hold them back from using their gifts to step into their leadership roles. Even in the face of adversity or when things were difficult, they stayed faithful to their calling. They inspire us to be bold, gracious, and filled with wisdom and humility. When we surrender our will to God and follow His lead for our lives, His power will strengthen us to stand up and use our voices to speak truth for what is good, beautiful, true, and righteous.

### Don't Play Small

*You don't have to play small or play it safe.*

Instead of playing it safe, they chose to full trust God, confident that He would guide their path and give them what they needed every step of the way. You know what, friend? He will do the same for you. You don't have to play small or play it safe. God is with you. He is for you. And by tapping into His power and strength, you can do all things.

Hey there, my beautiful friend! Can I just pour some truth into your heart right now? Stop shrinking back, stop playing small, and definitely stop letting those limiting beliefs keep you from stepping into the amazing calling God has for your life! Y'all, I've been there—wrestling with fear when I started Spark Media, or doubting if I was qualified enough when I wrote *The Struggle is Real: But so is God*, or wondering if anyone would even listen when I launched the By His Grace podcast. But here's what I know deep in my spirit: When God calls you to something bigger than yourself, He's already equipped you with everything you need to walk in that purpose.

Sweet sister, it's time to take that bold step of faith! Whether He's calling you to start that ministry, launch that podcast, write that book, or speak His truth from the stage—God's got you! He's right there, cheering you on, ready to show up in mighty ways when you say "yes" to His plans. So, come on, friend—let's stop playing it safe in the shallow end and dive deep into the adventure God has for you. Your voice matters, your story matters, and somebody out there needs exactly what God has deposited in you. Let's do this thing—together!

> *Sweet sister, it's time to take that bold step of faith!*

## Diverse Paths in Christian Leadership

God's vision for women leaders is not one-size-fits-all. Instead, it is as vast and diverse as the women He calls. Throughout the Bible, we see examples of women who led in various capacities—some in the public eye, others behind the scenes. What unites them is their unwavering faith in God and their commitment to His purposes. This uniqueness in women's gifts,

> *God's vision for women leaders is not one-size-fits-all.*

talents, and leadership roles underscores God's value and respect for each woman's distinct calling.

The beauty of these modern-day leaders is that they come from all walks of life. Look around, and you'll see God at work through women of every age and season of life. Some are raising families, others are climbing corporate ladders, and many are doing both. Their paths are as different as their stories.

A former corporate executive who felt called to leave her CEO position to start a ministry helping businesswomen integrate their faith and work life now leads workshops and mentoring programs while raising her three kids.

An artist and single mom began hosting Bible studies in her home studio with her unique way of teaching through visual art and storytelling, which grew into a thriving women's ministry that reaches thousands through social media and events.

A public school teacher who saw the need for teen mentorship in her community launched an after-school program that pairs high school girls with Christian women mentors, teaching life skills alongside Bible study.

A nurse practitioner who felt drawn to medical missions now splits her time between running a local clinic for uninsured patients and leading short-term medical global mission trips to the underserved.

A stay-at-home mom who discovered her gift for Bible teaching while leading her neighborhood mom's group returned to seminary in her 40s and now serves as a teaching pastor while homeschooling her children.

What matters isn't where they've been or what others think they should do; it's about following God's leading. These bold women aren't waiting for permission. Neither should you! They're stepping up, speaking the truth, and reshaping Christian leadership.

## Lessons for Modern-Day Leaders

The biblical examples of Lydia, Deborah, and Esther provide profound lessons for today's women leaders. Each of these ladies offers us timeless wisdom to encourage and guide us as we step into our God-given roles. Leadership rooted in faith is unshakable when grounded in God's eternal promises. Though Deborah, Esther, and Lydia each led in distinct ways, their stories share common themes that continue to inspire and instruct.

> *Leadership rooted in faith is unshakable when grounded in God's eternal promises.*

By examining the key components of their leadership, we can draw principles to apply to our journey. I encourage you to study their lives in the pages of Scripture as you lean into God's call for your life. Unlocking the principles exemplified by biblical leaders paves the way for effective and impactful leadership. These timeless insights provide a foundation for leading with purpose, integrity, and vision, enabling you to inspire and guide others with confidence and grace. By embracing this knowledge, you can apply it to the challenges and opportunities of the modern world.

## Courageous Faith

*True leadership is not defined by the absence of fear but by the presence of faith that overcomes it.*

Whether you're facing a challenging project, making a difficult decision, or stepping into a new role, remember that God goes before you. True leadership is not defined by the absence of fear but by the presence of faith that overcomes it. Like Deborah, a leader with courageous faith understands that battles are won on our knees. We have not because we ask not. Ask for God's leadership to guide and direct your path. Then go and do what He calls you to do with courageous faith.

Our leadership should be rooted in a deep faith, knowing God will fulfill His promises because He is faithful in completing the good work He has started in us. When you lead with courageous faith, you inspire others to trust God's promises and encourage them to act, too!

## Wisdom and Discernment

Wisdom listens first, then leads with clarity and conviction. Esther's leadership underscores the importance of seeking God's wisdom in decision-making. A wise leader knows when to speak and when to seek God's counsel in silence. This kind of leadership is not merely about knowing what to do but understanding why and when to do it.

A world filled with a cacophony of voices, social media, and Internet gurus, all vying for our attention, produces an endless drone of noise and distractions. It is crucial to seek quiet time and space to pray and listen for God's voice and His instructions. Even Jesus had to make time to get away from the crowds to hear His Father's voice. How much more do we need to make time for quiet and stillness away from the cares of this world to seek our Father's wisdom? Your leadership will be most effective when guided by the discernment that comes from a close relationship with God, spending time in His word, and taking the time to pray and listen for the Holy Spirit's guidance.

## Generosity and Service

Lydia's example teaches us leadership is about serving others and using our resources for the Kingdom. Whether you're running a business, leading a team, or serving a community, consider how you can use your finances and influence to bless others.

Leadership is not about hoarding power and resources but generously giving and serving selflessly to benefit others. A leader's true wealth is measured by the generosity they pour into others. Generosity is a mindset that multiplies impact. When you lead with an open hand, you inspire others to follow.

In my own leadership journey, I've discovered the more open-handed I am with resources at my disposal or opportunities that come my way, the more opportunities and resources come my way! People will often ask me, how did you get to do this or that with various opportunities I have had? Honestly, I don't hustle, grind, or seek after most of the opportunities; instead, the more open-handed I am, the more opportunities God brings.

My husband has taught me a lot about living a lifestyle of generosity. Watching him share his natural gift of generosity with others fills my heart with joy. His giving spirit inspires our entire family to open our hearts and hands to those around us. One of our family goals this year is to make a significant Kingdom impact by investing in the lives of others and using our financial resources within our church body and in our community.

We're helping fund several community projects, including a local culinary kitchen with a special mission. Not only will it provide meals for our homeless neighbors, but it also creates meaningful employment opportunities for those who need them most: single parents, veterans returning to civilian life, and survivors of human trafficking. The goal is to offer nourishing food and dignified work that helps people rebuild their lives.

Listen friend, the time has come to rise up and shine bright for Jesus. No more hiding your gifts, no more dimming your light, and no more letting fear hold you back from what God has called you to do. When you partner with the King of Kings, there's no limit to what He can do through your surrendered life. So take that step of faith today—even if your knees are shaking! When you step out in faith and walk in your calling, you'll discover a freedom and joy that makes you question why you waited so long. Now get out there and shine His light! The world needs what God has placed inside of you—you were created for such a time as this!

## APPLICATION QUESTIONS

Consider the examples of Deborah, Esther, and Lydia. How can their stories inspire you to step out in faith and lead with the courage and wisdom that comes from God?

........................................................................................................................

........................................................................................................................

........................................................................................................................

........................................................................................................................

........................................................................................................................

Reflect on the gifts God has given you. How are you currently using these gifts to serve others and glorify God in your leadership roles? What steps can you take to ensure that your leadership remains focused on stewardship and service rather than personal gain or recognition?

........................................................................................................................

........................................................................................................................

........................................................................................................................

........................................................................................................................

........................................................................................................................

Think of a situation where you need to exhibit courageous faith in your leadership. How can you trust God more in this area, knowing that He goes before you?

..................................................................................................

..................................................................................................

..................................................................................................

..................................................................................................

How can you cultivate a leadership style that inspires others to have faith in God's promises, especially during challenging times?

..................................................................................................

..................................................................................................

..................................................................................................

..................................................................................................

# PRAYER

*Lord,*

*We love you, and we praise you, and we come before You with hearts full of gratitude for the unique and powerful roles You have designed for women in Your Kingdom. We thank You for the biblical examples of Deborah, Esther, and Lydia, and others whose lives reflect Your wisdom, courage, and grace.*

*As we seek to understand and embrace our calling as women leaders, we ask for Your guidance, wisdom, and strength. Lord, we commit our work and leadership roles to You, trusting in Your promise that our plans will be established when we place them in Your hands. Help us to steward the gifts You have given us with humility and purpose, always seeking to serve others and bring glory to Your name.*

*Use us, Lord, as modern-day Lydias, Esthers, and Deborahs, to stand up for what is right, to guide others toward Your truth, and to make a lasting impact for Your glory. We dedicate our leadership to You, O God. Lead, shape, and use us according to Your perfect will. May everything we do be in honor of Your name.*

*In Jesus' mighty name, we pray, Amen.*

# Notes

# Navigating Respect and Authority

As I reflect on the journey God has taken me on in leadership, I'm reminded of the unique challenges and opportunities we face as Christian women in positions of influence. Whether you're leading a Fortune 500 company, running a ministry, or building a platform like I have as an author or in the podcasting world, you've likely experienced those moments where your authority was questioned, your voice was dismissed, or your calling was misunderstood.

I believe it is important for female leaders to know how to navigate respect and authority as a woman of faith in leadership. Let's explore practical strategies for standing firm in our calling without compromising our Christian witness. We can lead with both strength and grace—just as the Proverbs 31 woman did in her business ventures.

My prayer is that as you read these pages, you'll find encouragement to stop apologizing for the space God has called you to fill, lean into His wisdom to handle challenging situations with confidence, and have the freedom to fully step into the leadership role He has prepared for you. Because, sister, your leadership isn't an accident—it's an assignment from God Himself.

Let's explore together how to walk this path with wisdom, courage, and unshakeable faith.

# Scriptural Foundation

*"One day, as Jesus was teaching the people in the temple and preaching the gospel, the chief priests and scribes with the elders came up and said to him, 'Tell us, by what authority you do these things, or who it is that gave you this authority.'*

*He answered them, 'I also will ask you a question. Now tell me, was the baptism of John from heaven or from man?'*

*And they discussed it with one another, saying, 'If we say, "From heaven," he will say, "Why did you not believe him?" But if we say, "From man," all the people will stone us to death, for they are convinced that John was a prophet.'*

*So they answered that they did not know where it came from. And Jesus said to them, 'Neither will I tell you by what authority I do these things.'"*

~ Luke 20:1-8

*"And I sent messengers to them, saying, 'I am doing a great work and I cannot come down. Why should the work stop while I leave it and come down to you?'"*

~ Nehemiah 6:3

## Challenges Women Leaders Face

Women in leadership face unique challenges—some external, some internal. Among the most difficult is the ongoing struggle for respect in male-dominated spaces, which is frequently more complicated in the church space. Too often, women find themselves overlooked, underestimated, or forced to justify their position or seat at the table. While cultural shifts have opened many doors for women, many Christian women still wrestle with how to stand firm in their leadership while embodying Christlike humility and confidence.

> *Women in leadership face unique challenges—some external, some internal.*

The culture of many Christian organizations adds another challenge. Some institutions still hold traditional views on women's roles, requiring female leaders to navigate these spaces with wisdom and humility. Christian women in leadership often navigate a complex web of expectations—balancing biblical principles with the demands of modern leadership. The tension often arises from multiple, and sometimes unexpected, sources.

> *Christian women in leadership often navigate a complex web of expectations.*

Biblical interpretation plays a significant role. Christian traditions hold varying views on women's leadership. Some denominations emphasize submission while others celebrate strong female leaders like Deborah, Priscilla, and Lydia. Scripture offers examples of both, requiring women to prayerfully discern their calling.

Then there is the paradox of Christlike humility. Jesus modeled servant leadership and bold authority, washing His disciples' feet one moment and turning over tables while speaking with unwavering conviction in the temple the next. For Christian women, leading well means embracing this same tension—making decisive choices while maintaining a spirit of humility.

Humility and strong leadership are not opposing forces; they are complementary. Jesus showed us confidence is born from a secure identity in God, and humility makes room for His power to work through our weaknesses. When we embrace both, we lead with boldness, grace, and an unwavering trust in His purpose.

## The Challenge of Earning Respect

Women leaders frequently encounter skepticism regarding their capabilities. Whether it's being talked over in meetings, having their ideas dismissed until repeated by a male counterpart, or feeling the pressure to prove their worth, these struggles can be frustrating.

Scripture reminds us that godly leadership isn't about demanding authority—it's about walking in wisdom and integrity. Proverbs 31 showcases a woman who exercises business acumen, makes decisions, and manages resources with strength. Her actions speak for themselves. Likewise, our leadership should be rooted in excellence, leaving no room for doubt about our capabilities.

Leadership flows from competence, character, and intuition rather than external validation. The Proverbs 31 woman exemplifies this truth—she conducts business with wisdom and strength, letting her actions establish her authority. Modern women leaders can adopt this same principle: excellence in action speaks louder than words.

## Overcoming the Need to Justify Your Position

Many women feel the burden of proving they deserve their role or position. This can manifest as overworking, over-explaining, or over-apologizing. I know I've been guilty of feeling the need to over-explain or justify my leadership. I learned true confidence comes from knowing God has called me and He has called you—not just your credentials, experience, or work ethic.

Instead of constantly defending your leadership, let your work and character speak for themselves. Jesus never over-explained His authority; He simply led. When challenged, He responded with wisdom, not insecurity (Luke 20:1-8). In the same way, when faced with doubt, respond with clarity, not defensiveness.

*Instead of constantly defending your leadership, let your work and character speak for themselves.*

Many women leaders expend valuable energy proving their worth by working excessive hours to get respect and over-preparation for every interaction. They often feel the need to provide detailed justification of decisions or over-explain by throwing around their title and status, which often leads to frequent apologizing

However, true authority stems from embracing your calling with confidence. Jesus modeled this perfectly. He led with quiet assurance, responding to challenges with wisdom rather than defensiveness.

## Stop Over-Apologizing and Over-Communicating

Women leaders often feel the need to soften their words or over-explain their decisions to be accepted. However, constantly apologizing or offering excessive details can undermine authority. Avoid phrases like, "I'm sorry, but..." or "I just think that..." Instead, speak with clarity and assurance.

Your leadership decisions do not require permission or excessive justification. Be direct, be concise, and trust that God has positioned you for such a time as this (Esther 4:14). If an explanation is necessary, keep it brief and focused on the outcome rather than over-explaining the process.

*Your leadership decisions do not require permission or excessive justification.*

## Walking the Digital Divide

As the leader of Spark Media, I walked a unique path in the podcasting world—one that has brought both incredible opportunities and unexpected challenges. As a Christian leader in the podcast space, I often found myself straddling two worlds: the secular podcasting industry and the faith-based community.

I've been at industry conferences where secular professionals subtly dismissed my faith-based perspective. I have also sat in church buildings where church leaders struggled to embrace the digital ministry God called me to build or my calling as a women of faith to lead. Through it all, one truth has remained constant: our authority doesn't come from human validation; it comes from God Himself.

I am grateful for organizations like Focus on the Family and KHCB radio that supported my endeavors to amplify the voice of Christian podcasters. The men I encountered in these organizations treated me with professionalism and respect. For that I am eternally grateful.

## Pioneering Christian Podcasting

When I first stepped into the world of podcasting, I saw its immense potential for kingdom impact. I wanted to bring the best of what was happening in the podcast industry to my Christian author/speaker friends who were interested in podcasting. As I engaged with mainstream secular podcast industry professionals, it became clear that faith-based voices were often dismissed or excluded. Despite my success in building a strong platform and fostering a thriving podcasting community, I was often met with condescension, subtle censorship, and even rejection.

Industry professionals who championed diversity and inclusion often failed to extend that same courtesy to Christian voices. There were events where I was ignored, and moments where it was clear that my faith made me an outsider. I witnessed large secular organizations intentionally marginalizing conservative podcasters, creating barriers to visibility and access. Yet, I refused to compromise my message. Instead, I doubled down on my mission by creating platforms like the Spark Media Network to give Christian podcasters the support and recognition they deserved.

When God called me to step into this space of digital ministry and podcast leadership, I had no idea of the complexities I would face. Y'all, being a woman of faith in leadership while pioneering new paths in media isn't just about breaking one barrier; it's about facing challenges on multiple fronts.

On one side, there's this beautiful, traditional church structure that I deeply respect and love. But let me tell you, trying to help some church leaders see how God can use women, podcasting and digital media for His kingdom? That's been quite the journey. I've sat in meetings where my calling was questioned, not just because I'm using new technology but because I'm a woman stepping into leadership. Although, when I look back at how God used Spark Media to reach people for His kingdom, I see His faithfulness in every download, every testimony, and every life that was changed through that ministry.

The beautiful thing about serving the Lord in media is that it allows us to meet people right where they are—in their cars, during their workouts, or while they're doing dishes. This isn't about replacing traditional ministry. It's about expanding our reach for the Gospel in ways that complement what's happening in our churches.

What I've learned through it all is that when God gives you a vision, especially one that challenges the status quo, you must stand firm in what He's called you to do. Sometimes that means being the only woman in the room. Sometimes it means helping others see how digital platforms can be used for Kingdom work. But always, always, it means keeping your heart anchored in Scripture and your eyes fixed on Jesus.

## Navigating Church Leadership as a Woman in Media

Ironically, while the secular industry often dismissed me for being too Christian, I also faced challenges within the church. Many faith-based organizations, particularly traditional leadership structures, struggled to see the value of me as a woman in leadership and my digital ministry. Instead of embracing podcasting as a powerful tool for evangelism and discipleship outside of the church, some church leaders viewed it as less legitimate than traditional ministry roles.

At times, I was met with strong headwinds from church leaders who didn't understand my calling. Instead of support, I faced discouragement. Some, I believe, questioned the need for women in leadership roles while others simply didn't take podcasting seriously. It was frustrating to see the church miss out on the incredible opportunity to reach people where they already were—online, through audio and video content that could inspire and equip believers worldwide.

## Navigating Difficult Male Dynamics

Ladies, we can be assertive without being aaggressive. Jesus exemplified strength without arrogance. Women in leadership should adopt the same approach. Speak clearly, concisely, and with conviction, without feeling the need to prove yourself. We need to set clear boundaries and expect professionalism. It is essential to uphold respect in interactions. If a male colleague dismisses or interrupts you, politely but firmly reclaim the floor. "I'd like to finish my point before we move on."

Don't internalize disrespect. When faced with condescension, remember that how people treat you often says more about them than about you. Nehemiah faced opposition in his leadership, yet he pressed on because he knew his calling (Nehemiah 6:3). Likewise, stay focused on your purpose, not the opinions of others. Not all men are dismissive of female leadership. Many are allies who respect and support women leaders. Seek out those who uplift rather than those who undermine, and cultivate professional relationships built on mutual respect.

## Stand Firm

*At the end of the day, our validation does not come from human approval but from God.*

At the end of the day, our validation does not come from human approval but from God. Your leadership is not an accident. It is an assignment. If He has placed you in a position of influence, He will equip you to walk it out with grace, wisdom, and authority.

Whether facing dismissal from secular industry professionals or skepticism from church leaders, I remain unwavering in my mission to do what God calls me to do. At the end of the day, I don't look to the world or the church for validation. My calling comes from God. And when He opens doors, no one can shut them. Y'all, this journey has taught me that God's calling doesn't always come with a roadmap, but it always comes with His presence. And that's more than enough.

# APPLICATION QUESTIONS

In what ways have you felt the need to justify your leadership? How can you surrender that to God?

How do you handle situations where you feel disrespected in your leadership?

What practical ways can you exude confidence in your role while maintaining Christlike humility?

# PRAYER

*Heavenly Father,*

*Thank You for calling me to leadership. Help me to walk in confidence, knowing that my worth comes from You and not the opinions of others. Give me wisdom to navigate challenges, courage to stand firm, and grace to lead with humility. May my leadership be a reflection of Your love and truth.*

*In Jesus' name, we pray. Amen.*

# Notes

# THE MYTH OF THE "HUSTLE" AND RECLAIMING A GOD-CENTERED, CREATIVE LIFE

As a podcast host running a media company, I've had the incredible privilege of interviewing many inspiring guests—leaders, authors, and entrepreneurs doing amazing things for God's Kingdom. But there was a season in my podcasting journey when I felt utterly overwhelmed. Between planning a conference, acquiring speakers and sponsors, scheduling interviews, preparing content and social media, and managing the endless to-do list that comes with podcasting, I found myself running on fumes. I loved the work but was stretched thin. I hated feeling caught up in an endless cycle of constant hustle, trying to meet deadlines, and keeping up with everything that needed to be done at home, with family, and at work.

One day, I talked with a friend and exchanged stories about surrendering our busyness to God, and I felt a deep conviction in my heart. As I listened to her speak, I realized I had been so focused on producing content, growing my platform, and helping others do the same that I was neglecting the very reason I started podcasting in the first place: to glorify God and encourage others in their faith. I had let the demands of podcasting, teaching, and hosting conferences overshadow the joy and purpose of the calling.

I stepped back and prayed about how to realign my priorities. God reminded me of Ephesians 2:8-9: *"For by grace you have been saved through faith. And this is not your own doing; it is the gift of God, not a result of works, so that no one may boast."* It wasn't about how much I could produce or accomplish; it was about leaning into His grace and letting Him guide the process.

In the months that followed, I made some intentional changes. I started planning my podcast schedule with more margin for rest and prayer, batch recording, and content scheduling. I reminded myself that it was okay to say no to certain opportunities so I could focus on the ones God was clearly leading me to while giving myself some margin to play and rest.

As I dedicated my work to the Lord in prayer, I asked Him to use my work for His glory and put my trust in Him for the results. That season taught me an important lesson: Even when working in ministry or pursuing creative passions, it's easy to get caught up in the hustle and forget why we're doing it. But when we slow down, seek God's guidance, and work from a place of rest, we honor Him and find more joy and fulfillment in our actions. I needed to get back to my first love of spending more time with Jesus and creating out of an overflow of that time spent with Him.

## Scriptural Foundation

*"Be still, and know that I am God." Psalm 46:10*

*"And Asa did what was good and right in the eyes of the Lord his God. He took away the foreign altars and the high places and broke down the pillars and cut down the Asherim."*

**~ 2 Chronicles 14:2-3**

*"For by grace you have been saved through faith. And this is not your own doing; it is the gift of God, not a result of works, so that no one may boas."*

**~ Ephesians 2:8-9**

You frequently hear the rallying cries of "hustle harder," "rise and grind," or—I love this one— "You can sleep when you're dead." These mantras have deeply embedded themselves in the fabric of our culture, particularly in the realm of creativity, motivation, and entrepreneurship. They tell us we must outwork, outlast, and outperform everyone around us to achieve success. When we pause and reflect, we realize this lifestyle contradicts Christ-centered living. This endless pursuit of more—fame, money, and likes—drives us further away from the principles of grace, rest, and contentment that our faith teaches us.

When I first started writing and speaking, I attended a conference where I met a famous Contemporary Christian Artist. I asked her what advice she would give her younger self if she could go back in time. She said something to the effect of, "I would tell my younger self you don't have to be in all the places doing all the things." She said, "The Lord did more in my life when I met Him at the kitchen table than He did when I was trying to be in all places doing all things."

## Jesus' Example of Balance

In the Gospels, we see a picture of Jesus that starkly contrasts the frenzied pace of today's hustle culture. Jesus was never in a hurry. He moved with a sense of purpose and an extraordinary sense of peace and poise. Whether Jesus was teaching His disciples, healing the sick, or dining with sinners, He always took the time to be fully present in the moment. When people approached Him with urgent needs, He didn't dismiss them as interruptions to His schedule. Instead, He saw them as divine appointments. Even during His final hours, facing the agony of the cross, Jesus offered comfort to a repentant thief and made provisions for His mother's care.

In His life, we see the embodiment of Psalm 46:10: *"Be still, and know that I am God."* Jesus didn't rush through His earthly ministry because He operated from a complete alignment with His Father's will. He knew that actual effectiveness comes not from constant activity but from perfect obedience to God's timing. This divine sense of timing and purpose offers us a model for approaching our lives and vocations.

## The Dangers of Idolizing Productivity

*Instead of glorifying God through our work, we can risk turning our endeavors into idols.*

Instead of glorifying God through our work, we can risk turning our endeavors into idols. We bow down at the altar of productivity and sacrifice our spiritual, mental, and physical well-being. This grind culture, more often than not, results in burnout and creates a life out of balance. It sidelines what should sit at the center of our universe: our relationship with God and being present with those we love.

Idolizing productivity is a common pitfall in today's fast-paced world and can be particularly dangerous for women. The drive to achieve, to constantly do more and be more, can quickly become an idol that takes precedence over everything else, including spending time with Jesus, our health, and relationships.

In 2 Chronicles 14, we learn a valuable lesson from King Asa.

> *And Asa did what was good and right in the eyes of the Lord his God. He took away the foreign altars and the high places and broke down the pillars and cut down the Asherim and commanded Judah to seek the Lord, the God of their fathers, and to keep the law and the commandment. He also took out of all the cities of Judah the high places and the incense altars. And the kingdom had rest under him.*
>
> **~ 2 Chronicles 14:2-5**

King Asa did what pleased the Lord by removing idolatrous worship sites and leading the people of Judah to seek God and follow His commandments. He destroyed foreign altars and high places, ensuring that Judah focused on the true worship of the Lord. As a result, the kingdom experienced peace and rest during his reign.

Just as King Asa removed the foreign altars and high places to refocus Judah on worshiping the one true God, women must be vigilant in tearing down the idols of productivity that can distract us from our true purpose. When we allow the pursuit of productivity or anything else to dominate our lives, it becomes a form of modern-day idolatry, pulling our attention away from God and the things that truly matter.

Asa's example reminds us that we must lead intentionally, aligning our actions with God's will and ensuring that our focus remains on Him, not on the endless tasks that can so easily consume us. By doing so, we can create a space of peace and rest in our leadership, workplaces, and homes where God's presence is at the center, guiding our every decision.

By no means am I saying don't put in hard work! We should work hard and do everything with excellence. I am talking about a posture of the heart and idolizing our busyness and productivity. One day, I came to this hard realization when a church friend asked me how I was doing, and my response was, "I'm good, busy, but good." I realized I was always talking about how busy my life was. How often do we glorify our busyness instead of giving glory where glory is due? Jesus is the only one who is worthy. Extraordinary leaders learn to manage their time, schedules, and priorities wisely, making strategic decisions on when and where to put their focus.

## Biblical Wisdom on Work and Rest

The Bible gives us a healthier perspective. The Book of Ecclesiastes warns against endless toil for worldly gains, asking, *"What has a man from all the toil and striving of heart with which he toils beneath the sun?"* Ecclesiastes 2:22. In the New Testament, Jesus reminds us, *"For what does it profit a man to gain the whole world and forfeit his soul?"* Mark 8:36. Both passages challenge the worldly wisdom that advocates for unceasing hustle.

Instead, we should look toward the model God sets for us. He crafted the world in six days and rested on the seventh. Rest did not signify laziness or a lack of ambition on God's part; instead, it demonstrated completion and fulfillment. God saw what He had made and declared it "very good." We, too, should strive to cultivate a similar spirit of completeness in our work—doing all things to the best

> *The Sabbath is a gift from the Lord and the commandment we most often break.*

of our ability and recognizing the importance of rest and reflection. The Sabbath is a gift from the Lord and the commandment we most often break.

The world is noisy and chaotic, and our soul beckons us to come away with Jesus, where we cast our cares and delight in His presence. Sabbath rest is our reset from the cares of the world, where we can recharge. Resting and connecting with God actually helps us to be more productive when we do work. Jesus Himself often withdrew from the crowds to spend time praying and contemplating. He understood the value of solitude, of stepping back from His ministry to recharge and realign with His heavenly Father. If the Son of God saw fit to pause, should we not also find value in moments of stillness and rest?

## Realigning Priorities

Reclaiming a God-centered life involves evaluating our lives and realigning our priorities. Instead of endless scrolling on social media, chasing likes and retweets, and building platforms or sales figures, we need to create works

> *Reclaiming a God-centered life involves evaluating our lives and realigning our priorities.*

that glorify God and uplift others. Instead of measuring success by worldly metrics, we should find joy in well-done tasks, in being fully present, in the lives we touch, and in the moments when our work draws others closer to God. Essentially, we trade the fleeting rewards of the "hustle" for the enduring joys of a Christ-centered life.

To break free from the hustle culture, we must set boundaries, honor the Sabbath, and cultivate habits of rest and renewal. These practices do not make us more ambitious and more successful. On the contrary, they free us to do our best work—a work that honors God, blesses others, and brings genuine fulfillment to our lives.

*It's incredible how our creative spark returns when we slow down and let ourselves recharge.*

You know, sometimes we get so caught up in the daily hustle and grind that we don't stop to take a breather. There's something beautiful and healthy about accepting the gift of rest that God wants us to have. It's incredible how our creative spark returns when we slow down and let ourselves recharge. Plus, this deep sense of peace and joy bubbles up when we live the way we were meant to—not running ourselves ragged but finding that sweet spot of balance that God had in mind for us all along.

I recently made the difficult decision to resign from a leadership position. For weeks, I wrestled with the decision. After much prayer and seeking God's direction for what He wants in the next season of my life, I stepped down from my position with Influence Women. Whew! Let me tell you, this wasn't an easy choice at all, but my spirit has been sensing God moving me in a new direction for a while. I knew I needed to make this change to be at peace and in alignment with where He's leading me next. Sometimes, following His lead means making tough choices and stepping away from good opportunities to make room for His new opportunities and His best. I trust His plan and feel peace about this new season, and I'm excited to invest my time and energy in new places where I can serve His kingdom with intentionality.

I've been reflecting lately about leadership and purpose. You know those moments when you're rushing from one activity or meeting to the next, juggling a dozen different projects, and everything feels important? Sometimes, God gently taps us on the shoulder and asks us to pause. Not to stop leading, but to take a breath and look at where our heart and energy are flowing.

> *It's not about doing less. It's about doing what matters most*

It's like tidying up a cluttered room. When we step back and look at everything spread out before us, we can see more clearly the things genuinely matter and which ones we've just been carrying out of habit. Whether that ministry you've been pouring yourself into aligns perfectly with your calling, or something else tugging at your spirit deserves more of your attention.

The beautiful thing is that when we align our leadership with God's whispers and nudges, everything becomes sharper and more purposeful. It's not about doing less. It's about doing what matters most, what He's specifically called us to do. Sometimes, that means having the courage to say no to good things so we can say yes to the best things.

## Seeking True Validation

We must ask ourselves, "Whom are we trying to prove our worth to?" In the social media and digital connectivity world, it becomes easy to fall into the trap of seeking validation from our online audience. Each like, comment, and share offers a dopamine hit, a momentary affirmation that what we're doing matters. Yet, this is a precarious foundation upon which to build our self-worth. Today's viral sensation quickly becomes tomorrow's forgotten post, leaving us in a never-ending cycle of performance and approval-seeking.

Even beyond the digital realm, we can become consumed with winning the approval of colleagues, friends, or even family members. The temptation to win accolades and awards can be tempting. Scripture cautions us against such worldly validation.

Jesus implores us in the Sermon on the Mount, *"Do not lay up for yourselves treasures on earth, where moth and rust destroy and where thieves break in and steal, but lay up for yourselves treasures in heaven, where neither moth nor rust destroys and where thieves do not break in and steal."* Matthew 6:19-20

Remember, God's measure of our worth bears no correlation to the worldly values of success or social media metrics. The apostle Paul reminds us that our worthiness comes from our identity in Christ, not from our works or accomplishments.

He writes in Ephesians 2:8-9, *"For by grace you have been saved through faith. And this is not your own doing; it is the gift of God, not a result of works, so that no one may boast."*

## The Parable of the Prodigal Son

In the parable of the prodigal son, Jesus beautifully illustrates the concept of unconditional love and worth in the eyes of the Father. After squandering his inheritance, the son returns home not as a triumphant hero but as a broken man. Yet his father runs to him, embraces him, and celebrates his return. He doesn't chastise him for his failures or demand evidence of newfound productivity; he welcomes him back into the family.

This parable reminds us that our worth doesn't hinge on our performance. Our heavenly Father celebrates us simply because we are His children, created in His image. When we truly grasp this profound truth, it liberates us from the need to prove ourselves to others. We find freedom to work and create not for likes, accolades, or validation but for the sheer joy of glorifying God and serving others.

Imagine a life where you wake up each day fueled not by what you have to prove but by what you have to give. Imagine a creative practice rooted not in self-promotion but in self-sacrificial love. Friend, this is not a pipe dream; it's the life God calls us to embrace. To step into this life, we must dismantle the false idols of hustle and grind that we've erected in our hearts.

For too long, we've bought into the world's message that hustle and grind are the keys to success, and in doing so, we've erected false idols in our hearts—idols that demand our time, energy, and peace. I've realized that this relentless pursuit often leads us away from the rest and fulfillment God offers. We chase after achievement, believing that we'll finally be satisfied if we

> *True success is found in obedience to Him, not in the frantic pursuit of productivity.*

do more. But the truth is, this constant striving distracts us from the still, small voice of the Lord. I am committed to dismantling these false idols in my own life, surrendering the need to prove myself, and embracing God's rhythms of grace. True success is found in obedience to Him, not in the frantic pursuit of productivity. It's time we align our hearts and remember that His yoke is easy, and His burden is light.

## APPLICATION QUESTIONS

How does the "hustle culture" concept differ from the biblical principles of work and rest described in the Bible? Discuss the potential impacts of hustle culture on our spiritual, mental, and physical well-being.

............................................................................................................................

............................................................................................................................

............................................................................................................................

............................................................................................................................

............................................................................................................................

How does Jesus model a balanced approach to work and rest during His earthly ministry? How can we apply Jesus' example in our own lives and work?

............................................................................................................................

............................................................................................................................

............................................................................................................................

............................................................................................................................

............................................................................................................................

How can we reclaim a God-centered creative life in a world that often glorifies productivity and success? Share practical steps or habits to help us prioritize our relationship with God over worldly achievements.

...................................................................................................

...................................................................................................

...................................................................................................

...................................................................................................

...................................................................................................

What are some potential dangers of seeking validation from social media and otherworldly metrics? How can we shift our focus from seeking validation from others to seeking affirmation from God?

...................................................................................................

...................................................................................................

...................................................................................................

...................................................................................................

...................................................................................................

# PRAYER

*Heavenly Father,*

*We love you with all of our being. We come before You, grateful for the reminder that our worth is found not in our work or achievements but in our identity as Your beloved daughters. Help us escape the relentless rat race and find rest in Your presence. Teach us to balance our work with the peace and poise Jesus exemplified. Guide our creative efforts to honor You and to uplift those around us. May we seek Your affirmation above all else and find joy in fulfilling Your will. Grant us the wisdom to set boundaries, the courage to rest, and the grace to trust in Your perfect timing. In Jesus' name, we pray, Amen.*

# Notes

# CREATING BOUNDARIES AND AVOIDING BURNOUT

Burnout doesn't happen overnight. It creeps in slowly when you run fast and burn hot, especially if you are multi-passionate. You know those seasons where everything looks picture-perfect on the outside, but inside, you feel hollow, and you're running on fumes? I've walked through seasons of burnout, and let me tell you, it's not a badge of honor or proof of your dedication. It's a warning sign that something is desperately wrong and out of alignment. Have you been there, trying to pour from an empty cup? If you just pushed a little harder, stayed a little later, or said yes to one more thing, you could somehow achieve your goals and prove your worth.

*God didn't create us to run on empty.*

Here is the beautiful truth I learned during those dark days of burnout: exhaustion doesn't measure our worth. God didn't create us to run on empty. The Lord didn't design us to constantly sprint through life and gasp for breath. Oh no, sweet friend. He created us to thrive. The Lord has taught me that when we align our rhythm with His design for our life, we find our sweet spot of purpose and peace. But if we're not careful, we can let the demands of life, ministry, and business weigh us down, leading to exhaustion, overwhelm, and, eventually, burnout.

# Scriptural Foundation

*"And let us not grow weary of doing good, for in due season we will reap if we do not give up."*

~ Galatians 6:9

*"The wisest of women builds her house, but folly with her own hands tears it down."*

~ Proverbs 14:1

*"Come to me, all who labor and are heavy laden, and I will give you rest. Take my yoke upon you, and learn from me, for I am gentle and lowly in heart, and you will find rest for your souls. For my yoke is easy, and my burden is light."*

~ Matthew 11:28-30

## Work-Life Balance

Work-life balance has always been a challenge for me! I grew up a sturdy Midwestern girl and was taught the value of hard work. Fast-forward to getting married and raising kids. I quit my job consulting at Enron to raise and homeschool my boys. When my boys started growing up, I began praying about my life after homeschooling and began an entirely new career in my late 40s.

When I said yes to podcasting, I had no idea where it would lead me. When I answered the call to start Spark Media, I never planned on running a business or being a leader. My only goal was to be obedient and faithful to the call on my life.

In the past five years, I've written an award-winning best-selling Bible Study and collaborated on another book that launched at #1 on Amazon. I created four top-ranked podcasts, all ranked in the top 1-3 percent of podcasts globally, while helping hundreds of people launch and grow their own podcasts.

I have pioneered collaborations with other leaders in the faith, radio, podcast, and media space. I created countless opportunities to help the advancement of others, including creating a magazine to promote podcasters and give authors in my sphere of influence a place to be published. I launched a podcast network to help podcasters grow and monetize their shows.

I've hosted amazing retreats, workshops, and huge conferences and have taken the stage at many popular events. I am so grateful for the many incredible people I have met and had the opportunity to work with over the years. It has been a crazy, incredible journey. From the outside looking in, it looked like I was on top of the world. However, I came to a crossroads where I realized that all of the incredible things I was doing in business and ministry came at a high cost to my first love of being a wife and mom. It left me feeling frazzled, exhausted, and running on empty, and that's when I knew something needed to change.

As I prayed and asked God for wisdom, I heard Him say, "Turn your heart towards home." No one else can be a wife to my husband or a mom to my kids. I can't care for anyone else if I'm not caring for myself. I needed to find harmony in fulfilling my callings at work and home. This required me to say no to incredible opportunities that were good in one season but aren't the best for my current or future season. It's critical to understand the times, the seasons, and our assignments and capacity in each season. Scripture teaches that a wise woman builds her house, but a foolish woman tears it down with her own hands. Reflecting on this Scripture has prompted me to evaluate what is most important. I've learned that having boundaries is healthy and necessary to fulfill God's calling without burning out.

> *It's critical to understand the times, the seasons, and our assignments and capacity in each season.*

## Recognize the Signs of Burnout

> *Recognizing the early signs of burnout is vital so you don't crash and burn*

Recognizing the early signs of burnout is vital so you don't crash and burn like I did. If you recognize these early warning signs, you can take proactive steps to prevent them from worsening. These early signs can include physical exhaustion, emotional fatigue, and spiritual dryness.

Feeling weary and exhausted all the time, even after a good night's sleep, is a common early sign of burnout. Dragging yourself through the day and consuming copious amounts of caffeine to make it to the end of the day is another red flag. This fatigue can often feel like an overwhelming heaviness that lingers, making it difficult to focus or perform routine tasks.

You may also notice you're getting sick more often. This could be a sign your body is struggling to cope with the stress. The body's immune system can weaken due to chronic stress, leading to frequent colds, headaches, or other minor illnesses. During my season of burnout, at a routine check-up, I had my blood work checked and found out my adrenals were shot. My practitioner prescribed an adrenal supplement, and it has made a massive difference in my life.

You may also have difficulty falling asleep, staying asleep, or waking up feeling unrested. Despite exhaustion, the mind might be too active or anxious to allow for restorative sleep. Not sleeping can also be exasperated by menopause and perimenopause.

Losing enthusiasm for activities or tasks you once found fulfilling can also be a HUGE red flag. This includes feeling indifferent or disconnected from your work, ministry, or personal projects. Burnout can make you question your calling and purpose, leading to doubt and confusion about your direction in life.

> *Losing enthusiasm for activities or tasks you once found fulfilling can also be a HUGE red flag.*

If you start to wonder whether what you're doing really matters, it may be time to reassess your spiritual and emotional health. I experienced all of this during my burnout season. I even realized that I was super emotional and cried very easily—not my norm.

Friends, I wish I had seen the warning signs sooner. I remember the weeks leading up to our Spark Media Ignite Conference in the fall of 2023. I was spent, running on fumes, pouring every ounce of energy into making sure every detail for the event was perfect: every speaker lined up, every session planned, every attendee's experience prayed over and mapped out. But somewhere along the way, I lost sight of myself. The late nights, the constant emails, and the pressure to make it all come together took their toll on me physically and emotionally. I started feeling constantly drained, and my emotions were all over the place. I wasn't eating or sleeping well.

The joy I once felt in serving others became overshadowed by sheer exhaustion. My family could see the toll it took on me and asked me to quit everything. They didn't like seeing me so stressed and knew I needed a break. It wasn't until the conference ended that I realized how burned out I'd become. I knew I needed to step back, revaluate what was working, create boundaries, and allow God to refill my empty cup. I spent the remainder of the year taking better care of myself and making space for rest and renewal.

## Get Your House in Order

As I approached the close of 2023, I felt the Lord pressing this message heavily on my heart: "Get your house in order." Getting your house in order isn't just about tidying up our homes—though I admit, it's been on my mind more than usual, perhaps because I was in the midst of a remodel. But I sensed something deeper here that the Lord urges us to pay attention to as we build our lives.

In my quiet time, I'd been immersed in the book of Isaiah, and God pricked my heart with the words He spoke to Hezekiah: *"Set your house in order."* These words echoed in my spirit through Scripture, an email that crossed my path, and a prophetic message I heard. When God repeats Himself like that, I know it's time to take notice. It's like in the book of Revelation, where we repeatedly hear, *"He who has an ear, let him hear what the Spirit says to the churches."* Repetition in the Bible is a divine highlighter, ensuring we don't miss what God is communicating.

As women leaders, we are often pulled in many directions, balancing our work, ministry, and families. But as I've been praying about what it means to "get my house in order," I believe the Lord is calling me and us to a season of both physical and spiritual preparation. This means being intentional—more so than ever before—about the things that truly matter. It means letting go of distractions and prioritizing our lives to align more closely with God's will and His ways.

Sometimes, we're so busy building outside ministries, businesses, or platforms that we neglect the foundation that supports it all—our families and the spaces we inhabit daily. Throughout the following year, I felt God calling me to invest more intentionally in my home, nurturing it as a place of refuge, rest, and spiritual renewal for me and my family. For me, that meant simplifying, decluttering, and removing anything and everything that distracted me from my purpose and calling and didn't bring me joy.

Getting our houses in order goes beyond our physical spaces. It includes our spiritual and mental health and requires us to align our priorities and relationships as well. It's ensuring the people closest to you—your spouse, children, and loved ones—know they are cherished, valued, and supported. It's about taking the time to cultivate a healthy balance, ensuring that what we preach in public is lived out in private. When we do this, we can more fully step into God's calling with authenticity, strength, and integrity. God's order brings peace. When our homes reflect that, we are better equipped to lead, serve, and make an impact beyond our front doors.

I spent 2024 in a transitional season, sensing that God was doing something new in my life and ministry. I spent 2024 pruning my life, pulling away, quietly quitting, traveling with my husband, and spending more time being still and seeking His presence. Waiting on the Lord is not easy, especially for someone like me who loves to go and do.

But as I look ahead, I feel a strong call for discernment, obedience, and surrendering my will to His. It's about seeking His wisdom and walking in obedience, trusting that He is working all things together for good.

## 24/7 Availability and Factors Contributing to Burnout

> *A hurdle many of us face today is the expectation of constant availability.*

A hurdle many of us face today is the expectation of constant availability. My husband always tells me that I'm too available to people. He has done a great job managing digital communications on his terms, not falling prey to other people's urgency. The digital age, with its 24/7 news cycles and social media platforms, has increased the pressure to remain constantly "on." He calls social media the cruel mistress that always demands your attention, and it is the thing he despises most about my work.

We live in a world where the boundaries between work and personal life have become increasingly blurred, largely thanks to technology and our ability to work from home. Emails, social media messages, and urgent requests for counsel don't stick to a nine-to-five schedule. The constant influx of communication can make finding the time to rest, pray, recharge spiritually, or hear from God challenging, and leading to burnout.

Whether you are a woman in business, ministry, or a parent invested in the spiritual upbringing of your children, the demand for your attention and insight rarely pauses. Unlike the bygone era, when letters took weeks to reach their intended recipients, modern communicators find themselves bombarded by questions, criticisms, and demands for guidance at all hours of the day and night. People think texts and emails demand instant replies. But remember, even Jesus took time away from the crowds to pray and recharge. To avoid burnout, we need to make it a priority to carve out regular intervals for rest and spiritual refreshment.

> *To avoid burnout, we need to make it a priority to carve out regular intervals for rest and spiritual refreshment.*

## Financial Pressures can Play a Role in Burnout

Financial pressure adds a layer of stress that can contribute to burnout, too. It can add stress if you need to create income to support yourself or your family. Especially since the cost of living has increased so much, everything has gotten so expensive! It doesn't matter who you are. Everyone feels the squeeze. Concerns about money can become a source of significant stress, leading to concerns about job security, the future of ministry, and the ability to sustain your family, which can exacerbate burnout.

## Maintaining Integrity

Equally challenging is maintaining integrity while striving for broader relevance online. The culture wars entice us to take a stance on every controversial issue, often forcing us into contentious discourse with keyboard warriors if we are not careful. While standing firm in one's convictions is essential and remains a noble endeavor, keeping up with social media's demands can also be mentally and emotionally taxing.

> *I've learned that we don't need to comment on everything we see in the news or on social media.*

I've learned that we don't need to comment on everything we see in the news or on social media. Constantly scrolling through social media, or what my friend calls "doom scrolling," can lead to stress and anxiety. The urge to comment on every post or weigh in on current issues risks burnout, as the burden of constant vigilance can become overwhelming. A key to overcoming this challenge is staying calm, maintaining a solid grounding in biblical teachings, and setting boundaries regarding social media.

## Building Platforms and Chasing Metrics

Complicating matters even further is the pressure to expand our reach and impact, which fosters an obsession with metrics. Building platforms and chasing metrics often tempt us into a worldly concept of success. Whether it's someone starting a business, a writer trying to get a book deal, a preacher anxious about dwindling Sunday attendance, or a Christian vlogger concerned about subscriber counts, the quest for numbers and growth can lead to a kind of spiritual materialism that contradicts the teachings of Jesus.

Many people fall prey to the temptation to purchase followers to make themselves look more popular and successful, or even worse, start to believe their own hype. Girl, let me tell you something about believing your own hype—it's like quicksand for your soul. I've watched folks get so wrapped up in what the media says about them and what their followers say, that they start living in this bubble of awesomeness. Before you know it, they're nodding along to every compliment like it's gospel truth, forgetting all about the messy, real parts of themselves.

It's wild how fast you can lose touch when marinating in that praise juice. Those Instagram likes and media mentions? They're just telling part of your story, and typically only the shiniest part. The moment you start buying into all that glitter, you stop growing and learning, and that's when the real trouble begins.

Keep it real with yourself, flaws and all, because that's where the magic of being truly you lives. When we begin to judge our worth or the value of our message based on earthly measures of success, we stray from our true calling and our identity in Christ. We have value not because of our social media numbers, likes, and follows—we have value because we are image-bearers of Jesus Christ.

Finally, let's remember the emotional toll of living on the Internet and social media. Striving to measure up to everyone else's highlight reel can become emotionally and spiritually exhausting. Constantly chiming in to leave positive comments, give advice, or help guide people through life's storms is also emotionally laborious. This emotional weight often goes unnoticed but accumulates over time and can significantly contribute to burnout.

> *Striving to measure up to everyone else's highlight reel can become emotionally and spiritually exhausting.*

## Unrealistic Expectations

Finally, there's the burden of unrealistic expectations from oneself and others. There's often a perceived need to be always on and available to others. Striving to meet these lofty expectations can create a relentless cycle of overcommitment and disappointment, contributing to a sense of inadequacy and failure.

Avoiding burnout, therefore, requires a multi-faceted strategy. Practicing good time management, learning the power of no, and understanding that you can't respond to everyone and everything all the time are helpful practices. What has helped me from burning out is creating margins and setting up good boundaries with social media. Time blocking my calendar to manage and avoid over-commitment allows me to make time for what matters most to me, my family and those I serve. Like any other form of labor, spiritual work requires rest and recovery periods.

*Avoiding burnout, therefore, requires a multi-faceted strategy*

## Creating Guardrails for Social Media

As leaders and believers, we are responsible for speaking from a place of elevated consideration, especially regarding social media. When the world loses its ever-loving mind, we can become tempted to post things impulsively on social media out of frustration, confusion, pressure, fear, emotion, or the need to be correct.

Taking our thoughts captive and establishing a filter can help us predetermine how we want to present ourselves online and in the world. This involves deciding in advance how we wish to represent our brand, mission, or purpose, and creating guidelines for what we will and won't share on social media. Setting these boundaries simplifies the process of knowing what to post, ensuring that our content aligns with our values.

When it comes to social media and conversing with others online, uphold your convictions, but don't let the news or culture wars consume you. Try to avoid people and situations that ruffle your feathers. Reject worldly measures of success, and focus on being faithful to your calling and serving those in your sphere of influence. Invest in your emotional and spiritual well-being by taking regular breaks from social media.

Acknowledging these challenges is the first step in developing coping strategies, enabling a more sustainable approach to work-life balance. Whether that involves setting more explicit boundaries, seeking financial advice, or focusing on self-care, taking proactive steps can help alleviate the stressors that contribute to burnout.

By heeding these cautionary principles, you set yourself on a path to sustainable living. A candle only fulfills its purpose when lit, yet even candles need someone to protect them. Don't let your light flicker out because of burnout; remember, you have an essential role in guiding others and spreading the Light of the World.

## Don't Grow Weary

With every season, we choose where to focus our time, talents, and resources. My family has always been my number one ministry, but I've allowed running a ministry and business to take priority. Trying to be in all the places doing all the things is exhausting and leads to burnout. We must remember His yoke is easy, and His burden is light. Too many people quit because of weariness when they really need to stop and take a break.

> *With every season, we choose where to focus our time, talents, and resources.*

> *"And let us not grow weary in doing good, for in due season we will reap, if we do not give up."*
>
> **~ Galatians 6:9.**

The Apostle Paul stressed the importance of staying energized and doing good. As a modern-day Proverbs 31 woman, I often find myself stretched thin and teetering on the edge of physical and spiritual exhaustion. Can you relate? Burnout can become a perilous condition that undermines our families and ministries, shatters our motivation, and saps our spiritual vitality. By recognizing the signs of burnout and focusing on what matters most, we can keep our flames alive.

## APPLICATION QUESTIONS

What boundaries have you set in your life to maintain a healthy work-life balance? How effective have they been in preventing burnout? What changes might you need to implement?

...........................................................................................................

...........................................................................................................

...........................................................................................................

...........................................................................................................

...........................................................................................................

Share an instance when you felt close to burnout. What were the signs, and how did you address the situation? How can recognizing these signs early help you manage your responsibilities better?

...........................................................................................................

...........................................................................................................

...........................................................................................................

...........................................................................................................

...........................................................................................................

Considering your various roles, how do you prioritize your time and energy between your family and your ministry or career? How does your faith guide these decisions?

..................................................................................................
..................................................................................................
..................................................................................................
..................................................................................................
..................................................................................................

How has technology influenced your work-life balance? Discuss strategies to limit the negative impact of constant digital connectivity on your personal and spiritual well-being.

..................................................................................................
..................................................................................................
..................................................................................................
..................................................................................................
..................................................................................................

How do financial concerns and the emotional demands of ministry or career affect your stress levels? What practical steps can you take to mitigate these pressures while staying faithful to your calling?

...................................................................................................

...................................................................................................

...................................................................................................

...................................................................................................

...................................................................................................

# PRAYER

*Heavenly Father*

*We come before You, seeking Your wisdom and strength. Help us to establish healthy boundaries that honor You and sustain our well-being. Guide us to find rest in Your presence and to lean on Your promises when we feel overwhelmed. May Your Holy Spirit renew our minds and spirits, granting us the grace to balance our responsibilities with peace and joy. Thank You for being our constant refuge and strength.*

*In Jesus' name, we pray. Amen.*

# OVERCOMING FEAR AND EMBRACING COURAGE

I stood at the summit of a mountain just outside Jackson Hole, Wyoming, with my heart pounding, wondering how I'd gotten into this situation. Just hours before, I was full of excitement as our family embarked on a fun ATV adventure in the Grand Teton National Forest. I'm a "girlie girl" married to a rugged outdoor enthusiast, so I was determined to embrace this new experience with my husband and boys.

The journey up had been exhilarating – my youngest clutching my waist as we followed my husband's lead, climbing higher and higher into the majestic Tetons. The stunning views of the valley below took my breath away, but it wasn't until I realized I had to navigate back down that genuine fear gripped my heart.

Standing there, the wind whipping through my hair and my legs trembling, I was sure I'd be stranded forever on that mountaintop. That's when my husband's steady voice cut through my panic: "Keep your eyes on me. Just follow me and take it slow."

As we began our descent, I discovered a profound truth—I could manage each treacherous turn as long as my gaze remained fixed on him. The moment I looked at the steep drop-offs or tried to rely on my own limited experience, panic would threaten to paralyze me.

This mountain adventure became a powerful metaphor for my walk with God, especially during the intense spiritual battles of recent years. When He calls us to venture beyond our comfort zones, we naturally focus on the overwhelming circumstances surrounding us. But just as I made it down that mountain by concentrating on my husband's lead, we must navigate life's challenges by keeping our eyes fixed on Jesus.

> **God is positioning His daughters for such a time as this.**

God is positioning His daughters for such a time as this. He's calling us to be His voice, to impact our homes, families, and spheres of influence. The choice is ours. Will we let fear hold us back, or will we fix our gaze on Him and move forward in courage?

## Scriptural Foundation

*"Have I not commanded you? Be strong and courageous. Do not be frightened, and do not be dismayed, for the Lord your God is with you wherever you go."*

~ **Joshua 1:9**

*"Then you will know the truth, and the truth will set you free."*

~ **John 8:32**

*"Finally, brethren, whatsoever things are true, whatsoever things are honest, whatsoever things are just, whatsoever things are pure, whatsoever things are lovely, whatsoever things are of good report; if there be any virtue, and if there be any praise, think on these things."*

*~ Philippians 4:8*

## Overcoming Fear

In our journey as women leaders, fear often serves as a formidable barrier, casting shadows over our dreams and ambitions. Whether it's the fear of failure, the fear of the unknown, or even the fear of success, these anxieties can paralyze us and hold us back from stepping into the fullness of our God-given potential. Yet, Scripture reminds us time and again to *"be strong and courageous"* (Joshua 1:9). This isn't just a gentle encouragement; it's an exhortation and a call to action, a divine mandate and command to rise above our fears and walk boldly in faith.

Embracing courage is not about the absence of fear but the decision to move forward despite it. It's about standing firm in Christ's power and love in the face of adversity, knowing our strength comes not from our own abilities but from the One who gifts and calls us. Courage is an act of spiritual discipline—a practice of trusting in God's promises, leaning not on our own understanding but leaning into His strength when our faith falters.

> *Embracing courage is not about the absence of fear but the decision to move forward despite it.*

Boldness doesn't mean being loud or brash. It means standing firm in your convictions despite feelings of uncertainty, even when it's uncomfortable. It's about trusting that God's way is better, even when it doesn't make sense to others. Walking boldly in faith is about being rooted in truth and letting truth guide you every step of the way.

In this chapter, we will explore the nature of fear, how it manifests in our lives, and, most importantly, how we can overcome it through faith and love. We'll delve into practical steps to help build courage and resilience. Embracing our braveness will enable us to face challenges with a confident heart and an unwavering spirit.

## My Ongoing Journey to Be Courageous

Leading with courage has been an ongoing journey for me, one that God has called me to step into time and time again. When I launched Spark Media, I saw a need—a space where Christian communicators could amplify their voices and impact the world with the message of faith. It was uncharted territory. The uncertainties were real, but I knew God had placed this vision on my heart.

I was pleasantly surprised by the incredible open doors and connections God orchestrated. Still, I was sadly disappointed by other leaders who wouldn't even give me the time of day. Sadly, there is a lot of competition in both the secular and the Christian writing, speaking, and podcasting spaces. However, I stepped out in faith with God's guidance, trusting that He would provide the way. You know what? He blessed my obedience by doing far more than I ever imagined!

Standing firm in my convictions has been another area where I've had to lead with courage. When a podcast industry event canceled one of its sponsors simply due to the presence of one of the network's hosts at the event, along with the values they represent, it compelled me to make the hard decision to walk away from the event and refrain from attending future gatherings. I understood it meant losing potential connections, but I couldn't compromise my beliefs. Sometimes, courageous leadership involves standing alone for what is right, even when it's inconvenient. I've come to realize that doing the right thing is often doing the hard thing. That might be why the road is narrow that leads to life.

> *Standing firm in my convictions has been another area where I've had to lead with courage.*

Courage also looks like stepping into leadership roles that stretch us. Over the years, I've organized and spoken at many events where I've shared the message God has placed on my heart. Through each success and failure, these opportunities required me to speak with passion and conviction. It is not always easy, but I've learned that courage grows when we trust God to show up. The more I rely on Him and less on my notes, the better I do.

Finally, pioneering in the Christian media space has required tremendous courage. Building Spark Media and creating events like the Spark Conference, Spark Bold Business, or Mama Bear Rising—Faith Over Fear Powered by Spark Media, there was no blueprint for such events. These were bold steps of faith. I believe when God calls us to something, He equips us, but that doesn't mean it won't stretch us.

Stepping down from Spark Media to step into the COO role at Trilogyworks was not an easy decision either. Spark Media has been a labor of love, a platform where I poured my heart into empowering Christian communicators to amplify their voices.

Stepping into this new season with my husband Peter to grow Trilogyworks is a drastic change, but it is also a testament to the very principles I teach other creatives and communicators—obedience, courage, and boldness in following God's calling. This transition allows me to apply the skills and experiences I've gained to a broader mission, driving growth, innovation, and impact at Trilogyworks. Leadership often requires letting go of one season to embrace the next, and I trust God to guide my steps as I lead with faith and purpose in this new role.

I've embraced the challenge, knowing that true courage means stepping out, even when the path isn't clear. Leading with courage isn't about having it all together. It's about obeying God's will and His call on your life, trusting Him to illuminate the path, and encouraging others to walk boldly in their God-given calling.

## Stepping into Leadership with Faith, Confidence, and Love

Stepping into the unknown can feel daunting, especially when combined with the added pressures of leadership. Authentic leadership isn't about having all the answers or never making mistakes; it's about being willing to step forward, take risks, and lead others with humility and integrity. As a woman of faith, your leadership is grounded in your relationship with God. When you submit your endeavors and leadership roles to God, He will guide your steps and open doors that no one else can. He has specific doors just for you to walk through with divine plans and purposes.

Fear often holds us back from stepping into the fullness of what God has called us to do, but Scripture reminds us that there is no room for fear when we are rooted in God's love. Love is the way to drive out fear! I've also had to overcome fear and repeatedly step out in faith— from early in my corporate career, to homeschooling, to starting a whole new career of writing, speaking, podcasting, trailblazing in the media space, and starting a business in mid-life.

> *Fear often holds us back from stepping into the fullness of what God has called us to do,*

Although overcoming those challenges has been difficult, some of the greatest fears I've faced have arisen during my journey as a parent. Whether it was deciding to give life to my son, whom the doctors advised us to abort because he was deemed incompatible with life, or trusting God's plan for my special needs son while wondering who will care for him when I am no longer around.

Sometimes, the enemy of our souls can really twist us up. Out of my deep love, care, and concern for my children, I often let fear hold me back too much. Worried about whether they will get hurt or make poor choices, I've tried to protect them. But many times, I likely parented out of fear instead of with wisdom. My husband often says to let them fail because God teaches us valuable lessons during tough times. We must lean on Him to see us through. The Lord has graciously revealed these fears and has kindly worked through me to learn to trust in His love for our children and His sovereign plan for our family, even when I don't fully understand.

As 1 John 4:18 says, *"There is no fear in love, but perfect love casts out fear. For fear has to do with punishment, and whoever fears has not been perfected in love."* It's not through our strength or courage that we overcome fear but through the power of God's love flowing in and through us.

When we bravely step into the fullness of what God has in store for us and embrace the truth of His perfect love, which is greater than any fear we may encounter, we find peace in His presence. God's love frees us from the limits of fear and encourages us to walk confidently in the purpose He has designed for us. When we lead with love—whether in our businesses, with our families, or in the places God calls us to lead—we can be assured that fear will find no place to take root.

*Love is the most powerful weapon God has entrusted to you for conquering fear.*

Love is the most powerful weapon God has entrusted to you for conquering fear. When your heart is filled with His love, you can lead without hesitation, confident that His love will dispel any doubts or anxieties that may try to invade your thoughts. We can move forward boldly, trusting that God's love will clear the path and eliminate every fear along the journey. As we courageously embrace all that God has for us, His perfect love drives out fear.

## Using Our Gifts to Love and Serve Others

A practical way to embrace leadership is by identifying your unique strengths and considering how they can be used to love and serve others. Reflect on the gifts God has given you—whether it's a talent for design, a passion for writing, or a knack for problem-solving. Contemplate how you can apply your God-given gifts and talents to lead in your community, workplace, or business. Leadership doesn't always mean being the loudest or most visible. Often, it's about being faithful in small matters, following God's lead, serving others, and leading by example.

Many women grapple with doubts about their abilities and the worth of their contributions. Fear and insecurity often cause them to question whether they are "good enough" or if they can truly make a difference. These doubts can paralyze you, hindering your progress toward the positions God has designed and ordained for you. Friend, the world needs you to show up and illuminate the unique light that only you can shine—boldly and brightly. Scripture encourages us to overcome these doubts by placing our trust in God and His sovereign plan. God has equipped you with everything you need to succeed—not just talent but also power, love, and the discipline required to fulfill what He's called you to do and to lead effectively.

## What We Think, We Become

Our thoughts are powerful. They shape our perceptions, influence our emotions, and drive our actions. If you want to change your life, you need to evaluate what you are consuming in the form of media, entertainment, and the words of others. Most important is learning to control your thought life and change the negative patterns that hold you back from living your best life. We can't continue to think the same negative thoughts and expect different outcomes.

*Our thoughts are powerful.*

The enemy's lies come in the form of doubt, discouragement, disappointment, distraction, fear, and the like. With the Lord's help, we must identify the lies holding us back by taking our thoughts captive, enabling us to be intentional in our thought lives. We must always compare our thoughts to the truth of Scripture because our mindset shapes our reality. What we think and what we let control our minds and thoughts are what shape us and ultimately drive us.

It is more than just positive thinking; it's about aligning our thoughts with God and who we are in Him.

Philippians 4:8 has served as a filter to help me monitor my thought life; I know it can help you too!

> *Finally, brethren, whatsoever things are true, whatsoever things are honest, whatsoever things are just, whatsoever things are pure, whatsoever things are lovely, whatsoever things are of good report; if there be any virtue, and if there be any praise, think on these things.*

When a thought enters your mind, ask yourself: is this true? Is it honest or just? Is it pure, lovely, virtuous, or praiseworthy? If not, we must take these thoughts captive and prevent them from taking root in our minds. We can't allow our minds to dwell on doubt, discouragement, or lies. If we constantly focus on negativity, fear, and doubt, we will live in a state of perpetual anxiety and defeat. This will impact both our physical and emotional well-being. My mom was a bit of a Nervous Nelly, and I spent much of my formative years watching her emotions spiral out of control. I witnessed the toll it took on her physical body, manifesting as debilitating arthritis that wracked her body with pain. She nagged and complained about everything, which greatly affected her overall demeanor and disposition.

Proverbs 14:30 ESV says, *"A tranquil heart gives life to the flesh, but envy makes the bones rot."*

Conversely, when we meditate on goodness and God's promises, we cultivate a mindset of victory and peace. When we fill our minds with God's truth, truth overpowers the lies. Each of us has a mental tape that plays repeatedly in our heads. This tape is often filled with lies we've believed about ourselves, our circumstances, and our future.

But God's truth has the power to silence those lies. We can rewrite those tapes when we choose to conform ourselves to God's image.

## Identifying and Replacing Negative Thought Patterns

The first step in renewing our mindset is to identify the negative thought patterns that have taken root in our minds. These patterns often manifest as self-doubt, fear, and hopelessness. Once identified, we must actively replace them with God's truth.

> *The first step in renewing our mindset is to identify the negative thought patterns that have taken root in our minds.*

John 8:32 reminds us, *"Then you will know the truth, and the truth will set you free."* When we immerse ourselves in Scripture and allow God's truth to permeate our minds, we break free from the chains of deception.

Here is a practical exercise to help identify and replace your lies. The practice of journaling has personally helped me sort out my thoughts and feelings and helped me focus on what is good, lovely, and true. It has also helped me to pray for things beyond my control.

Record your thoughts and feelings in a journal. Spend a week writing your recurring thoughts and ensure you are honest and thorough. Next, evaluate your thoughts and review your journal at the end of the week. What patterns do you notice? Were they harmful or positive, life-giving or destructive? Find Scripture to counter each negative thought, then replace those thoughts with the truth of Scripture and begin meditating on those truths. Write the verses next to the corresponding thoughts and meditate daily on these Scriptures to renew your mind. Renewing our minds isn't a one-time event; it's a daily discipline. Just as we need daily nourishment for our bodies, our minds require daily spiritual sustenance. I like to post Scripture all around my house to remind me of God's love and His great promises.

## Overcoming Imposter Syndrome

I recently had a conversation with a friend who called me for encouragement because she struggles with Imposter Syndrome. Imposter Syndrome is a common struggle, especially among those stepping into new roles or responsibilities. It is the nagging feeling that you are not good enough, that you are a fraud, and that you will be exposed at any moment. This destructive mindset can cripple you and try to stop you from succeeding. It contradicts what God says about us.

*Imposter Syndrome is a common struggle, especially among those stepping into new roles or responsibilities.*

When those emotions rise, we must remind ourselves of who we are in Christ and who He created us to be. When we feel like imposters, it is time to remind ourselves of our identity in Christ so that we can push back the fear and step out boldly in faith.

If you have a dream in your heart and feel God calling you to step out of your comfort zone to try something new, take that step. It doesn't need to be perfect; you will learn along the way. Step out boldly in faith. Do it afraid. Trust the process and don't despise humble beginnings. Do the work and

*Do it afraid.*

leave the outcome to the Lord. His plans for you are greater than you realize, and you will never experience the abundance of the Lord if you don't try.

Another practice that may help you is to write down affirmations based on Scripture to counter feelings of inadequacy, such as "God chooses me," "I am equipped for every good work," and "God's strength is made perfect in my weakness." I began this practice when I wrote *The Struggle is Real: But so is God*. This was a game-changer for my spiritual walk.

Pray daily, asking God to reinforce the truth of Scripture in your heart and mind. Confront imposter syndrome with the truth of God's Word. Cultivate a mindset rooted in confidence and purpose, knowing God's chosen and equipped us for every good work He has prepared for us to walk in.

## Embrace a Renewed Mindset

Girl, it is time to embrace a new mindset! If we want to succeed in our leadership journey, we must renew our minds, which is not a one-and-done situation. It is a daily fight and an ongoing journey of surrender that leads to profound transformation. We must be gatekeepers of our thought life and be intentional with the thoughts we dwell on. By aligning our thoughts with God's truth daily and taking our thoughts captive, we can experience the fullness of life He intends for us.

> *Girl, it is time to embrace a new mindset!*

Remember, "What we think, we become." Therefore, it is essential to guard our minds and keep a gate on what we allow to enter into our

> *"What we think, we become."*

minds. This includes the music, television programs, and podcasts we listen to or watch, the places we go, and the company we keep. I've heard it said that we are the sum of the five people closest to us, which is why we must guard our inner circle, too.

I am thankful for the people in my life who love Jesus, practice having a heart of gratitude, are purpose-driven, and have a growth mindset. I'm inspired by uplifting content and people who are actively growing in their faith. I am blessed to be surrounded by family and friends who love Jesus and who inspire me to become the best version of myself.

With God's help, we can walk in the fullness of our calling and become all He created us to be. We are transformed as we renew our minds by reading, studying, meditating, and applying God's Word to our lives. When we begin to see ourselves and our circumstances through the lens of God's truth, this perspective empowers us to live victoriously. Embrace the journey of renewing your mindset daily, and watch God work wonders in your life.

## Now is the Time!

> *It is never too late to step into the calling God has placed on your life.*

It is never too late to step into the calling God has placed on your life. No matter where you find yourself today, God's purpose for you remains steadfast and unchanging. Don't let fear or doubt hold you back from becoming all that He created you to be. I didn't know what I didn't know when I first started, but I didn't let that stop me. I didn't let fear hold me back from what I knew God called me to do; I stepped out and learned along the way. It doesn't mean I didn't experience fear; on the contrary, I did it afraid. The path ahead may seem daunting, and the challenges may feel overwhelming, but remember that God equips those He calls. Your unique experiences, talents, and passions have prepared you for this moment. Trust in His timing, and boldly move forward, knowing He is with you every step. Do it afraid. Embrace the courage to pursue your God-given calling and watch how He will use your obedience to make a lasting impact in your life and on those you influence.

## Seven Practical Steps You Can Take Today to Build Courage and Resilience

### 1. Acknowledge Your Fears

The first step in overcoming fear is to recognize and name it. Pretending it doesn't exist only gives it more power over you. By identifying your fears, you bring them into the light where they can be tackled instead of letting them fester and grow. Once you call out your fears and shine a light on them through prayer and reflection, you can allow God to transform them into opportunities for growth. Acknowledging your fears is the first step toward overcoming them. Feeling apprehensive when faced with the unknown or entering a new role is natural, but these feelings don't have to define or limit you.

It's essential to identify the fears that are holding you back—whether it's fear of failure, rejection, or feelings of inadequacy—and present those thoughts to God in prayer. When you acknowledge your fears, you open the door for God to work in your heart, replacing your fear with His peace, love, and strength. Remember, courage isn't the absence of fear, but the choice to move forward in spite of it. It means moving past the fear to do it afraid. Trusting in God's power is perfected in your weakness. So let Him transform your fears into a testimony of His faithfulness.

*Facing our fears takes courage.*

Facing our fears takes courage. When we try to ignore them, they often grow stronger in the shadows of our minds. Instead, try to identify what's really making you anxious. It could be starting a new job, moving to a different city, or taking on a leadership role.

Once you name these fears through quiet reflection and prayer, you can begin to see them differently, not as roadblocks but as opportunities to grow stronger in your faith.

2. **Anchor Yourself in Scripture**

God's Word is a wellspring of courage, and it is our daily bread. Meditate on Scriptures that speak of God's strength and promises, and let these truths sink deep into your heart. Verses like Isaiah 41:10: *"Fear not, for I am with you; be not dismayed, for I am your God; I will strengthen you, I will help you, I will uphold you with my righteous right hand."* These truths remind us that we are never alone in our battles. God is always with us—our source of courage and strength. But you must be connected to the source to access the power.

3. **Surround Yourself with a Supportive Community**

Courage is contagious. Surround yourself with like-minded women who will encourage, pray, and walk alongside you as you face your fears. A supportive community helps to provide the wisdom and strength we often lack on our own. When you are part of a church community or tribe that lifts you up, prays with you, and speaks truth into your life, you are

*Courage is contagious.*

reminded that you are not alone in your journey. Connecting to a community is essential to help you find the courage to pursue and thrive in your calling.

This network of support can help you navigate challenges, celebrate victories, and stay grounded in your purpose. Whether it's a small group, a mentorship circle, or a close-knit circle of friends, these relationships are vital for building resilience and courage. Together, you can draw strength from one another, share wisdom, and spur each other on to boldly step into the roles God has called you to. Remember, we are stronger together. Having a community of faith-filled women by your side can make all the difference as you pursue your God-given dreams.

### 4. Practice Small Acts of Bravery

Courage is built over time through small, obedient, consistent acts. Begin with little steps that take you outside your comfort zone. With every step, you find taking the next one easier. Practicing these minor acts of bravery is a powerful way to build the courage you need to pursue your God-given calling. No matter how small the step is, each one you take is a victory over fear.

It could be as simple as speaking up in a meeting, reaching out to a potential mentor, or taking a step toward a new project that's been on your heart, like writing a book or launching a podcast.

*Courage is built over time through small, obedient, consistent acts.*

These small acts of bravery stack up, strengthening your confidence and resilience bit by bit, making you more courageous with each step. Each time you push past your comfort zone, you grow bolder, become more equipped, and prepare yourself for the challenges ahead. In these seemingly small moments, your faith trains your heart to trust God more deeply, leaning on His strength rather than your own. By consistently practicing courage daily, you're building the spiritual muscle needed to tackle the larger tasks God has in store for you. Remember, bravery isn't just a one-time leap—it's a habit you cultivate through intentional, small steps of faith.

5. **Reflect on Past Victories**

Taking time to remember how God has brought you through challenges previously, and reflecting on His faithfulness in the past, gives you the courage to trust Him with your future. Reflecting on past victories is a powerful way to fuel your boldness as you step into new challenges. When you take the time to remember the moments when God has been faithful in your life—those times when He helped you overcome obstacles, answered prayers, or guided you through difficult seasons—you build a foundation of trust that empowers you to move forward with confidence.

> *Take twelve men from the people, from each tribe a man, and command them, saying, 'Take twelve stones from here out of the midst of the Jordan, from the very place where the priests' feet stood firmly, and bring them over with you and lay them down in the place where you lodge tonight.*
>
> ~ Joshua 4:2-3.

We are forgetful, so it is essential to record God's faithfulness. Remembrance stones reminded the Israelites of God's faithfulness and power and became a memorial for future generations of God's miraculous works. I love journaling my prayers and recording God's answers. Going back through my old journals is a constant reminder of God's faithfulness. Each past victory is a testament to God's unwavering presence and His ability to work all things for your good.

> *We are forgetful, so it is essential to record God's faithfulness.*

By recalling these moments, you remind yourself that the same God who brought you through before will do it again. This reflection strengthens your faith and emboldens you to take the next step, knowing that God is with you and will continue to lead you. So, as you face new opportunities and challenges, let your past victories inspire you to be bold, trusting that the God who brought you this far isn't finished with you yet!

## 6. Develop a Resilient Mindset

Resilience is bouncing back after setbacks. We all make mistakes and fail sometimes. Our ability to bounce back from these setbacks helps us to develop grit and a resilient mindset. When we train our minds to see challenges as opportunities for growth rather than insurmountable obstacles, we can move forward more quickly.

> *Resilience is bouncing back after setbacks.*

Resilience is about enduring the trial and thriving in adversity. Developing a resilient mindset is vital for every woman who wants to lead and step into her God-given calling. It is not a matter of if but when. Life will bring challenges, setbacks, and unexpected twists. How you respond to them will shape your journey and be your guide. Oftentimes, our response is the only part of life we can control.

Grit is about pressing forward with unwavering faith, even when the road gets tough. It's choosing to see obstacles as opportunities for growth and leaning on God's strength to persevere through every trial. The path forward is about building a strong foundation through daily prayer and Scripture, finding people who share your faith, and rewiring your thoughts with God's truth. When life gets stormy (and it will!), these anchors keep you steady. Every time you meditate on His promises, it's like adding another layer of strength to face whatever comes your way.

Remember, resilience is also built by trusting God's plan and His timing, knowing that He's using every situation to refine you and prepare you for more extraordinary opportunities. Embrace life's challenges with a spirit of determination, confident with Jesus as your best friend, and you can rise above any difficulty to fulfill the purpose He has set before you.

7. **Lean on God's Strength, Not Your Own**

True courage comes from relying on God's power to carry you through. When you feel weak or emotions rising in you, it is time to turn to Him in prayer, casting all of your burdens on Him. Courage is a journey, not a destination. It's a narrow path you walk daily with the Lord, and each step draws you closer to becoming the fearless woman God created you to be.

> *True courage comes from relying on God's power to carry you through.*

Trust in the Lord, embrace the journey, lean on Him, and let His courage guide you.

## APPLICATION QUESTIONS

Identify your fears. What specific fears are currently holding you back in your leadership journey? How do these fears manifest in your thoughts and actions? Take time to reflect on these and bring them to God in prayer.

........................................................................................................................

........................................................................................................................

........................................................................................................................

........................................................................................................................

........................................................................................................................

What negative thought patterns do you need to identify and replace with God's truth? How can you use Philippians 4:8 as a filter to evaluate and renew your thought life?

........................................................................................................................

........................................................................................................................

........................................................................................................................

........................................................................................................................

........................................................................................................................

What small, practical steps can you take this week to step outside your comfort zone? How will you trust God to build your courage and resilience in these moments?

..................................................................................................

..................................................................................................

..................................................................................................

..................................................................................................

..................................................................................................

Who in your life can you lean on for encouragement and prayer as you navigate your fears? How can you intentionally cultivate a supportive community around you?

..................................................................................................

..................................................................................................

..................................................................................................

..................................................................................................

..................................................................................................

# PRAYER

*Heavenly Father,*

*Thank You for the strength and courage that comes from Your presence in our lives. We ask that You help us recognize and overcome the fears that try to hold us back from fully embracing the roles and destiny You have called us to. Fill our hearts with Your peace and our minds with Your truth. Guide us as we step out in faith, knowing that You go before us and that Your strength is made perfect in our weakness.*

*Surround us with people who will uplift and encourage us and help us inspire others through our testimonies of courage and faith. May our leadership reflect Your love and glory, and may we walk boldly in the purpose You have set before us.*

*In Jesus' mighty name, we pray. Amen.*

# DISCERNING GOD'S VOICE

Discerning the voice of God is a necessary lifeline for the days we are living in. We are living in crazy, challenging times, and hearing from the Lord is crucial for us to discern the truth and to provide us with wisdom on how we should live. We must learn to tune our hearts and minds to the still, small voice of the Holy Spirit and seek His wisdom daily.

*Discerning the voice of God is a necessary lifeline for the days we are living in.*

As I've leaned in to listen to the Lord this year, I've discovered the power of intentional stillness. I've created space for more deliberate moments of quiet with the Lord in prayer and His Word. Choosing to step away from the constant barrage of news and social media has refreshed my soul. Whether driving silently in my car or enjoying meals alone, I've learned to embrace solitude. These moments of stillness have deepened my awareness, allowing me to be more fully present while living the life God has called me to live intentionally.

Hearing God's voice provides a crucial lifeline in these challenging times. Discerning His truth and wisdom guides our daily decisions and shapes our path. The need to tune our hearts to the Holy Spirit's gentle whispers will be more critical in the days ahead as we face a deluge of deception.

## Scriptural Foundation

*"All Scripture is breathed out by God and profitable for teaching, for reproof, for correction, and for training in righteousness, that the man of God may be complete, equipped for every good work."*

~ 2 Timothy 3:16-17

*"And it shall come to pass afterward, that I will pour out my Spirit on all flesh; your sons and your daughters shall prophesy, your old men shall dream dreams, and your young men shall see visions."*

~ Joel 2:28

*"The heavens declare the glory of God, and the sky above proclaims his handiwork."*

~ Psalm 19:1

*"My sheep hear my voice, and I know them, and they follow me. I give them eternal life, and they will never perish, and no one will snatch them out of my hand."*

~ John 10:27-28

Leadership and purpose flow from hearing God's guiding voice and obeying His commands. Yet questions often arise: Are these thoughts our own or divine promptings? When our hearts stir, what is their source? Even amid doubt, our Good Shepherd gently guides us back to His path.

> *Leadership and purpose flow from hearing God's guiding voice and obeying His commands.*

In this chapter, we'll explore how God communicates with us. Understanding these divine methods is essential for us to be leaders who hear from God, and empower us to influence and impact others.

## God Speaks to Us Through His Word

God speaks to us primarily through the Bible, His Word. It is His love letter to us. The Bible is our guidebook to truth. It is an instruction manual for daily living containing everything we need to know from Him.

Second Timothy 3:16-17 declares, *"All Scripture is breathed out by God and profitable for teaching, for reproof, for correction, and for training in righteousness, that the man of God may be complete, equipped for every good work."*

The Scriptures are God's voice speaking directly to us. Have you found verses that give you just what you need when you need them? God's words are faithful to us when we search for them. It can feel like "He said that just for me"

> *The Scriptures are God's voice speaking directly to us.*

when we find answers to questions or need affirmation to make it through the day. Other times, the Word we receive in our quiet time is for someone else, and circumstances will arise in our day to apply it.

Scripture is God's primary voice—His love letter and guidebook for daily living. His words meet us precisely when needed, speaking directly to our circumstances. Sometimes, these revelations serve others, surfacing at the right moment in our day to minister to someone else's needs.

## The Spirit's Guidance

The Holy Spirit dwells within believers, influencing our conscience and providing revelation—our divine helper who helps us understand and live out Scripture's teachings. Through the Spirit's power, God speaks directly to us and through others, sharing wisdom that builds up the Church. When receiving counsel, an open heart balanced with scriptural discernment ensures we remain grounded in truth.

He may also direct us through the work of the Holy Spirit. As born-again believers, the Holy Spirit resides within us when we put our faith and trust in Jesus. The third person of the Trinity, the Spirit of God, our helper, can influence our conscience. Our Spirit contains the Holy Spirit, who helps us hear and understand the more profound things we can't fully comprehend.

The Holy Spirit is our comforter and guide; through His power, we can understand and live out what Scripture teaches. God can speak to us through His voice and the voices of others, imparting wisdom that encourages and edifies the Church. We are not only recipients of this divine counsel but also channels for it. We should choose our words carefully when speaking into one another's lives to ensure they reflect truth based on Scripture. When advice is given, let us accept it with an open heart while verifying its truthfulness against what Scripture teaches!

## Reading and Meditating on God's Word is Paramount to Understanding Truth!

We've got to be in The Word so that it can permeate our very being and we can detect any falsehood or slightly twisted truth by others. Staying rooted and grounded in the Word will help serve as the lens we use to interpret the world. God speaks to us in many ways, from the pages of our Bible to the still, small voice within. God's Word is an invaluable tool with eternal wisdom to guide our lives.

Through careful observation and study of God's Word, we can discern His voice amid the many competing messages in today's world. We don't simply open the Bible to find a verse that aligns with what we want to hear regarding staying in a job, starting a new one, or various other situations. Instead, we engage with the Word daily and observe how God's messages are conveyed in the context of the many ways He communicates with us. It is essential to read the chapter and verse in context to understand to whom it is addressed and the original intent of the Scriptures.

Regular immersion in Scripture helps us detect subtle distortions of truth. God's Word provides the lens through which we interpret the world.

*God's Word provides the lens through which we interpret the world.*

## Discerning God's Voice Through our Circumstances

Amazing things can happen when we are open to the Holy Spirit's nudging and act according to Christ's character. Our seemingly random encounters can be divinely inspired, leading us down a path that only God could have opened up! We never know how our acts of kindness will impact those around us. Something as simple as helping someone get gas or giving an elderly person assistance can mean more than meets the eye. These random acts of compassion ripple outward with profound results often seen only when we look back on a situation later on.

## Listening to God's Voice

God speaks to us in various ways, including through His Word, prayer, and the counsel of others. He also speaks through the Holy Spirit, other believers, our circumstances, dreams, and through His creation.

> "My sheep hear my voice, and I know them, and they follow me. I give them eternal life, and they will never perish, and no one will snatch them out of my hand."
>
> ~ John 10:27-28

As you seek to set business goals and make plans, listen intentionally to God's voice. This might involve spending time in Scripture, fasting, praying, seeking the guidance of trusted mentors, or simply being still before God in prayer. Be open to the ways God might speak to you, whether through a verse that resonates with your situation, a word of wisdom from a mentor, or a sense of peace in your spirit. He is our Great Shepherd who leads and guides us. We grow in our leadership by spending time in God's Word, praying, and listening to discern His voice. He is speaking; are you listening?

## Hearing From God

Hearing from God is not just a skill—it's a vital spiritual discipline that we, as Christian women leaders, must cultivate through regular practice and obedience. In pursuing our calling, we must stand firm in our faith, rise with courage, and lead with unwavering conviction. God's voice is our guide. As we tune our hearts to His frequency, we align ourselves with His purpose, enabling us to lead with clarity, wisdom, and boldness.

## God Speaks to Elijah

God speaks to us in the ordinary routines of life. Often, it is not the significant events in life where we hear His voice; instead, it is in the daily rhythms of life, as seen in the way God spoke to Elijah.

> *God speaks to us in the ordinary routines of life.*

> *There, he came to a cave and lodged in it. And behold, the Word of the Lord came to him, and he said to him, "What are you doing here, Elijah?" He said, "I have been very jealous of the Lord, the God of hosts."*
>
> *For the people of Israel have forsaken your covenant, thrown down your altars, and killed your prophets with the sword, and I, even I only, am left, and they seek my life, to take it away." And he said, "Go out and stand on the mount before the Lord." And behold, the Lord passed by, and a great and strong wind tore the mountains and broke in pieces the rocks before the Lord, but the Lord was not in the wind. After the wind came an earthquake, but the Lord was not in the earthquake. After the earthquake, there was a fire, but the Lord was not in the fire. And after the fire, the sound of a low whisper.*

Did you catch that? He didn't speak through the earthquake, wind, or fire. He spoke to Elijah in a whisper. And, just like Elijah, if we want to hear from God, we must quiet ourselves and listen to His whispers.

## God Speaks to Us in Dreams

God communicates with us in many ways, and dreams are one of them. We may receive insights into our lives and the world around us through our dreams. We can gain insight into ourselves and God's divine will by paying attention to our dreams. *"And it shall come to pass afterward, that I will pour out my Spirit on all flesh; your sons and your daughters shall prophesy, your old men shall dream dreams, and your young men shall see visions."* Joel 2:28

Dreams can also provide spiritual guidance and remind us to stay on track with God's life plan. We may receive warnings or encouragement from God through our dreams to help us make important decisions or take necessary steps toward achieving His desires.

*God may be communicating with us through our dreams.*

Have you ever had a dream that seemed so real that it felt like God was speaking to you when you woke up? God may be communicating with us through our dreams. Dreams are often seen as a way for God to talk to us more directly and powerfully. Dreams can be interpreted in many ways, but some believe they can be used as divine communication. Dreams can contain messages from God or even warnings about what will happen.

In Genesis 41, Joseph interpreted Pharaoh's dream and saved Egypt from famine. Similarly, God may use dreams to guide or warn us about our lives. God speaks to us through dreams in many ways, whether through symbols, visions, or words. We must pay attention and interpret them correctly to understand the message He is trying to convey appropriately.

## God Speaks Through Creation

One of the most influential and profound ways God speaks to us is through his creation. Psalm 19:1 exalts, *"The heavens declare the glory of God, and the sky above proclaims his handiwork."* We can see God's love and care for us in the beauty of nature, our body's complexity, and the universe's wonder. We can feel God's presence in all He has made whenever we walk through a forest or look up at a star-filled night sky.

From star-filled skies to mountain majesty, creation testifies to our creator. These natural wonders offer solace, inspiration, and reminders of His care. By being observant, we can understand more deeply how much God loves and cares for us. We can find peace and hope in the natural world around us and be inspired by the beauty and complexity of His creations. For some, this is seen in the majesty of mountains. For others, it is sandy beaches or beautiful sunsets.

## Affirmation and Confirmation from Others

Discerning God's voice often comes through affirmation and confirmation from others, as He frequently speaks through the people He places in our lives. When we prayerfully seek His guidance, God may use trusted mentors, friends, or even unexpected encounters to confirm the direction in which He is leading us. These affirmations will align with His Word and resonate deeply with the Spirit within us, providing clarity and peace. While it is essential to weigh these confirmations against Scripture, the counsel of others can serve as a powerful reminder that God's plans are rarely intended to be pursued in isolation. Instead, He invites us into a community where the voices of fellow believers echo His truth and help us discern His will more clearly.

## A Word of Warning

*Messages bombard us through media, relationships, and daily life.*

Messages bombard us through media, relationships, and daily life. Evaluating these inputs against Scripture protects us from distorted truth. While social media can inspire faith, it shouldn't replace personal engagement with Jesus through His Word and prayer. Words hold immense power, so discerning truth is crucial. We must evaluate the messages we receive from others, including what we take in through movies, music, or social media. What may sound good, right, or even pleasing can sometimes distort reality—that's why discerning the truth from lies is crucial.

You can be encouraged by what you see on social media, as it can inspire and uplift you in your walk with Christ. However, it's essential not to let these glimpses of others' faith journeys replace your relationship with Jesus.

Don't settle for a secondhand account or interpretation of Jesus based on what you see online or someone else shares. Instead, make it a priority to directly engage with His Word. Pick up your Bible and read the words of Jesus for yourself. Spend time in personal worship and prayer; seek to experience Jesus firsthand. Seeking His presence is the prize, and our personal connection with Him will deepen our faith, providing a foundation that goes beyond the fleeting moments shared on social media.

To take a stand as leaders, we must be deeply rooted in God's Word, sensitive to the Spirit, and courageous in action. This journey requires us to move forward in faith, even when the path ahead is unclear, trusting that God is directing our steps. Let us seek His voice with all our hearts, listen intently, and act decisively. In doing so, we will lead others and fulfill God's unique calling. Stand firm, dear sister, for God is with you, and His voice will guide you every step of the way.

## APPLICATION QUESTIONS

How do you distinguish between personal thoughts and God's voice in leadership decisions?

..................................................................................................

..................................................................................................

..................................................................................................

..................................................................................................

..................................................................................................

..................................................................................................

When has the Holy Spirit guided you beyond your understanding?

..................................................................................................

..................................................................................................

..................................................................................................

..................................................................................................

..................................................................................................

..................................................................................................

Describe a time God spoke through ordinary circumstances.

..................................................................................................................

..................................................................................................................

..................................................................................................................

..................................................................................................................

..................................................................................................................

..................................................................................................................

Have meaningful dreams shaped your spiritual journey?

..................................................................................................................

..................................................................................................................

..................................................................................................................

..................................................................................................................

..................................................................................................................

..................................................................................................................

# PRAYER

*Heavenly Father,*

*Open our hearts to hear Your voice in the depths of our souls. Thank You for Your living Word that lights our path and Your Spirit who guides our steps. Grant us wisdom to recognize Your whispers amid life's noise. Sharpen our discernment through Scripture, Your Spirit's promptings, and creation's testimony. Help us distinguish truth from distortion and follow Your leading with courage. Keep us still before You, listening for direction. May our leadership reflect Your glory and grace.*

*In Jesus' name, we pray. Amen.*

# BUILDING A FOUNDATION OF FAITH

Do you know how they say you need a solid foundation when building a house? Well, girl, it's the same with life—except that foundation is Jesus! When I first started Spark Media, I remember talking about walking into the great unknown. I had zero idea what I was doing, if I'm being honest.

But here's the thing. I didn't need a fancy business plan, I had something way better. I had my prayer journal, worn-out Bible, and the Creator of the universe as my chief collaborator and business partner. Every day, I'd sit there with my coffee and Bible, asking, "Alright, Lord, who should I reach out to, and what do you want me to do today? And, y'all, even when things got messy (and trust me, they did!), I just kept coming to Him, seeking His wisdom, and trusting He was in control. When you build your life on God's foundation, you can walk through any door He opens, knowing He's got your back.

# Scriptural Foundation

"Everyone then who hears these words of mine and does them will be like a wise man who built his house on the rock. And the rain fell, the floods came, and the winds blew and beat on that house, but it did not fall, because it had been founded on the rock. And everyone who hears these words of mine and does not do them will be like a foolish man who built his house on the sand. And the rain fell, and the floods came, and the winds blew and beat against that house, and it fell, and great was the fall of it."

~ Matthew 7:24-27

"Unless the Lord builds the house, those who build it labor in vain. Unless the Lord watches over the city, the watchman stays awake in vain."

~ Psalm 127:1

"Whatever you do, work heartily, as for the Lord and not for men, knowing that from the Lord you will receive the inheritance as your reward. You are serving the Lord Christ."

~ Colossians 3:23-24

## The Rock-Solid Foundation

It's easy to get swept up in the whirlwind of trends, strategies, and quick fixes. Every guru has a product or a course promising to solve all your problems. True success isn't just about algorithms, metrics, or market strategies; it's about building on the firm foundation of Jesus Christ. Our call as Christian women leaders is not to chase fleeting success or the latest trends. Our mission is to build something far more lasting and impactful on the solid rock of Jesus Christ. The world is hungry for and desperately needs women rooted in their faith, unwavering convictions, and bold leadership. When you show up in faith to lead, your wisdom, leadership, and guidance can inspire, motivate, and leave a lasting impact on those you lead.

> *It's easy to get swept up in the whirlwind of trends, strategies, and quick fixes.*

Just as the wise man in Matthew 7 built his house on the rock, we must establish every aspect of our leadership based on Christ's teachings. This foundation will keep us firm, no matter what storms we face—economic downturns, societal pressures, or personal challenges. Only what we build on the foundation of Christ will stand the test of time.

As we navigate the complexities of leadership, Psalm 127:1 reminds us that unless the Lord builds our endeavors, all our efforts will be in vain. *"Unless the Lord* builds the house, those who make it labor in vain. Unless the *Lord* watches over the city, the watchman stays awake in vain. Therefore, let this chapter be your guide to making faith the cornerstone of your leadership so that every decision, action, and strategy is aligned with God's purpose for your life and those you lead.

## Aligning Leadership with Christian Values

*Leading with faith isn't just a nice idea, it's a game-changer.*

Leading with faith isn't just a nice idea, it's a game-changer. When I started making decisions with God as my CEO, everything shifted. I had the ultimate collaboration partner! It's amazing to see how bringing your faith into your work doesn't just help the bottom line—it lifts everyone and shows them what's possible when you put God first. And let me tell you, nothing beats watching those you impact grow stronger because they know they're part of something bigger.

## Integrity: The Cornerstone of Trust

Since Spark's founding, I've had to make some difficult decisions, some of which have considerably impacted my business and personal life. Because I feel deeply, I also hurt deeply. Not everyone will understand the personal sacrifices you have to make as a leader or the reasons behind your decisions. I've done my best to let Romans 12:18 guide me when misunderstandings occur. *"If possible, so far as it depends on you, live peaceably with all."* You cannot control other people's perceptions of you and your decisions. You can only control your words, actions, and responses.

*Integrity must be at the heart of your leadership.*

Integrity must be at the heart of your leadership. Proverbs 11:3 declares, *"The integrity of the upright guides them, but the crookedness of the treacherous destroys them."* As leaders, we must be examples of honesty, transparency, and fairness. In a world where cutting corners is often the norm, our commitment to integrity sets us apart and establishes trust with those we lead. This trust is more than just nice; it is essential for building a strong, unified team that shares your vision.

## Empowering Others

Jesus showed us that true leadership is about serving others. *"The greatest among you shall be your servant."* Matthew 23:11. As women leaders, we have the unique opportunity to model servant leadership in every aspect

> Jesus showed us that true leadership is about serving others.

of our work and empower others. We prioritize the well-being of those we lead, foster an environment of respect, and empower others to reach their full potential. By putting others' needs above our own, we create a culture where everyone can thrive, powerfully reflecting Christ's love. One of the greatest joys in my work with Spark Media was connecting with others and watching their relationships flourish. You've probably heard the expression, a rising tide lifts all boats, and it is true. You rise when you uplift others.

## Excellence as a Standard

When we set excellence as the bar for ourselves and others, we create an atmosphere that pleases the Lord. We should do everything with excellence because we serve the King of the Universe with our work. In everything we do, we should offer God our very best. Colossians 3:23-24 calls us to work with all our heart as if working for the Lord. *"Whatever you do, work heartily, as for the Lord and not for men, knowing that from the Lord you will receive the inheritance as your reward."* Excellence in leadership is about giving our best in everything we do—decision-making, team management, and strategic planning. This pursuit of excellence honors God and inspires those we lead to strive for their best, creating a ripple effect of positive influence.

## Faith-Fueled Decision-Making

*Leadership entails making difficult decisions.*

Leadership entails making difficult decisions. It's easy to rely on worldly wisdom or popular opinion. Often, doing the right thing and the hard thing are the same. Being a leader who honors Christ means our decisions should be infused with prayer and guided by faith and a biblical worldview. When we allow God's truth to shape our leadership, we make wise decisions that align with His purpose. Often, this may look different than we expect. For instance, think about how Jesus would approach a challenging personnel decision.

In Luke 22:42, Jesus defers His will to the will of the Father, saying, *"Father, if you are willing, remove this cup from me. Nevertheless, not my will, but yours, be done."*

When we consider Christ's words and actions, this can lead to decisions that are not only fair but also reflect the love and compassion of Christ.

## Trusting in God's Provision

As leaders, we are stewards of the resources God has entrusted to us—our time, talents, and finances. This stewardship requires us to manage these resources wisely, but it also calls us to be generous. In leadership, generosity can take many forms, from investing in your team's growth to giving back to your community.

> *As leaders, we are stewards of the resources God has entrusted to us—our time, talents, and finances.*

Every leader knows that with leadership comes uncertainty. Yet, we must remember to trust God's provision in these moments. As Matthew 6:33 reminds us, when we seek first the kingdom of God, He provides all we need. This trust empowers us to lead boldly, knowing that our ultimate security comes from God, not our circumstances.

I experienced this firsthand when planning the Spark Media conference during the pandemic. Despite the uncertainties, I leaned into prayer, seeking God's guidance every step of the way. The result was a powerful gathering that united a new generation of podcasters with established voices in Christian broadcasting by partnering with the National Christian Broadcasters to host my event. It was a testament to how faith can turn uncertainty into an opportunity for God's glory.

## Balancing Stewardship and Generosity

While it's essential to be prudent in managing resources, we must also remember that we are called to be cheerful givers (2 Corinthians 9:6-8).

> *By leading with generosity, you bless others and model a life that reflects God's abundant grace.*

In your leadership, look for ways to give back—whether through charitable donations, mentoring others, or supporting causes that align with your values. By leading with generosity, you bless others and model a life that reflects God's abundant grace.

Our faith shouldn't be compartmentalized; it should be woven into every aspect of our leadership. Here are some practical steps to ensure that your faith stays at the core of your leadership.

## Define Your Mission and Values

Your leadership should be based on a clear mission and values that reflect your faith. These guiding principles will help you remain true to your calling, even when challenges arise. At Spark Media, our mission was to amplify content that offers biblical solutions and inspiration, changing the world one podcast at a time. What is your mission? How do your values influence the way you lead?

Defining your mission and values is an essential investment that lays the foundation for your organization's long-term success. A clear mission provides direction and purpose, acting as a guiding compass for every decision and initiative. Core values establish the principles by which your organization operates, fostering a culture of integrity, consistency, and trust. When clearly articulated, mission and values inspire and unify your team and communicate your purpose to clients, stakeholders, and the community. This alignment ensures that everyone is working toward a shared vision, creating a strong, purpose-driven organization capable of thriving in any environment.

## Cultivate a Culture of Prayer

Prayer is the foundation of strong leadership. Encourage your team to pray regularly and make prayer a part of your decision-making process. When we invite God into our leadership through prayer, we open the door for His wisdom and guidance to direct our path. Let your faith guide every aspect of your leadership—from making decisions to interacting with your team. Uphold integrity and strive for excellence in all you do, reflecting the character of Christ in your leadership.

> *Prayer is the foundation of strong leadership.*

Don't be afraid to let your faith shine in your leadership. Whether through sharing a Scripture, offering a word of encouragement, or simply leading by example, let your light be a testament to the power of faith in leadership.

Christian women leaders have a unique opportunity to empower others. By building our leadership on the foundation of faith, we can create a lasting impact, lead with integrity, and inspire others to follow in Christ's footsteps. Remember, the world is watching, and our leadership can be a beacon of hope, strength, and godly wisdom in a world that desperately needs it.

## APPLICATION QUESTIONS

Reflect on the foundation of your business or personal life. Is it built on the rock of Christ, or are there areas where you feel it may be on shaky ground? What steps can you take to strengthen your foundation?

.................................................................................................

.................................................................................................

.................................................................................................

.................................................................................................

.................................................................................................

In what ways does your leadership practice reflect your Christian values? Are there areas where your actions might not fully align with your faith? What changes can you make to align these areas?

.................................................................................................

.................................................................................................

.................................................................................................

.................................................................................................

.................................................................................................

Think about a challenging business decision you've recently faced. How did your faith influence that decision? If faith wasn't a factor, how might the outcome have been different if it had been?

..............................................................................................................

..............................................................................................................

..............................................................................................................

..............................................................................................................

..............................................................................................................

What practical steps can you take to fully incorporate your faith into the foundation of your brand or business? Identify one change you can make this month to enhance the visibility of your faith in a professional context.

..............................................................................................................

..............................................................................................................

..............................................................................................................

..............................................................................................................

..............................................................................................................

# PRAYER

*Heavenly Father,*

*We come before You with hearts full of gratitude for the wisdom and guidance You have given us. Thank You for reminding us of the importance of building our lives and businesses on the solid rock of Your Word. As we seek to align our business practices with Your divine principles, we ask for Your continued presence and direction in all we do.*

*Lord, help us to be wise builders, constructing our leadership philosophy on the foundation of faith that will stand firm against any storm. May integrity be the cornerstone of our endeavors, and may our actions always reflect the love and truth of Christ. Give us the courage to serve others selflessly and to pursue excellence in all things, knowing that our ultimate reward comes from You.*

*We surrender our plans and ambitions to You, trusting that You will provide all we need as we seek Your kingdom and righteousness first. As we move forward, may our mission and values be rooted in Your truth, and may our faith be evident in every decision we make. Grant us the wisdom to navigate challenges with grace and to trust in Your provision even when the path ahead is unclear. Strengthen our resolve to honor You in all aspects of our business so that we may leave a lasting legacy that glorifies Your name.*

*In Jesus' mighty name, we pray. Amen.*

# ALIGNING VISION AND STRATEGY WITH GOD'S PURPOSE

I know leaders whose vision is locked in and others who excel at strategy, but it is rare to find a leader who combines vision and strategy and aligns them with God's purpose. God calls us to stand up, remain steadfast in our courage and convictions, and boldly walk in the vision God has placed on our hearts and execute it with purpose and passion.

The world desperately needs strong, capable women deeply rooted in God's purpose. Women who rise with conviction, clarity, and courage to lead with grace and authority impact and empower other women. This chapter will guide you in developing a vision that aligns with God's will and empowers you to lead confidently, inspiring others to do the same.

> *The world desperately needs strong, capable women deeply rooted in God's purpose.*

# Scriptural Foundation

*"And the Lord answered me: 'Write the vision; make it plain on tablets, so he may run who reads it.'"*

~ Habakkuk 2:2

*"Where there is no prophetic vision the people cast off restraint, but blessed is he who keeps the law."*

~ Proverbs 29:18

*"If any of you lacks wisdom, let him ask God, who gives generously to all without reproach, and it will be given him."*

~ James 1:5

## The Power of Vision in Leadership

> **Vision is the lifeblood of effective leadership.**

Vision is the lifeblood of effective leadership. It illuminates the path forward, ensuring every decision and action is intentional and aligned with God's purpose. Proverbs 29:18 reminds us that without vision, people lose their way. This is true in our personal lives, businesses, and leadership. A lack of vision leads to confusion and misalignment, while a God-inspired vision brings clarity, purpose, and a strong sense of mission.

As you develop a vision for your brand, ministry, business, or leadership, let it reflect the deeper purpose that God has placed within you. What is the ultimate goal you hope to achieve? How do you want to impact the world? As Christian leaders, our vision must be anchored in God's will and His grand plan for our lives. Take time to seek His guidance, allowing Him to shape your vision according to His purposes.

## Pray for Divine Wisdom and Strategy

God's ways are the best! James 1:5 calls us to seek God's wisdom, promising He will generously provide it. As you craft your strategic plan, bathe each step in prayer. Ask God to reveal His will for your leadership, ministry, or business, and be open to the unexpected paths He may lead you down. God's plans often surpass our understanding, leading us in directions we didn't foresee but that are ultimately for our good and His glory.

> *God's ways are the best!*

Seeking wise counsel during this planning stage is also crucial. Proverbs 15:22 highlights the value of wise advisors. Surround yourself with mentors, partners, and fellow believers who will speak life into your vision. Their wisdom, rooted in God's truth, will offer valuable insights and encouragement as you move forward. They can provide a different perspective, challenge your assumptions, and help you see

> *Surround yourself with mentors, partners, and fellow believers who will speak life into your vision.*

blind spots in your plan. Together, you can navigate the complexities of leadership with confidence and faith.

## Trusted Advisors

A circle of trusted advisors and accountability partners is one of the most valuable assets you can cultivate in both your personal and professional life. These individuals provide wisdom, guidance, and perspective that help you navigate challenges, make informed decisions, and stay aligned with your goals. No one succeeds in isolation; we all have blind spots and areas where we can grow. Trusted advisors bring diverse experiences and insights, offering constructive feedback and innovative ideas to take your leadership, business, or ministry to the next level.

Accountability is equally vital because it ensures you remain consistent and disciplined in pursuing your goals. When left to our own devices, it's easy to drift off course or justify compromising our commitments. However, when you're accountable to a trusted group of individuals, you are far more likely to follow through. They provide the encouragement needed to keep going when things get tough and the gentle correction required when you veer off track. This structure fosters a culture of growth and integrity, helping you remain true to your values and calling.

A circle of trusted advisors also serves as a sounding board for your ideas, offering insights that challenge you to think critically and refine your plans. These relationships often foster creativity and innovation as your advisors push you to consider perspectives you may not have otherwise explored. They also provide a safe space to be vulnerable, admit weaknesses, and seek guidance without fear of judgment. This openness leads to personal and professional development as you allow others to pour into your life and sharpen your skills.

Accountability relationships are compelling because they not only support your growth, they demand it. Knowing that you must report your progress, share your struggles, or update others on your commitments creates a healthy sense of responsibility. These relationships hold you to a higher standard and encourage you to reach for excellence. They remind you that you are not walking your journey alone and that your decisions impact those around you.

A circle of trusted advisors and accountability partners ultimately reflects humility and wisdom. Surrounding yourself with individuals willing to speak truth into your life and hold you accountable is a sign that you value growth over comfort and integrity over convenience. It's an investment in yourself, your mission, and your legacy, ensuring you have the support and guidance to fulfill your God-given calling.

> *A circle of trusted advisors and accountability partners ultimately reflects humility and wisdom.*

## The Role of Prayer in Leadership

Prayer is not just a foundational step; it is the ongoing connection that sustains and empowers us in leadership. It is a direct line to God, where we align our thoughts with His, seeking His guidance and strength. Prayer is not merely about asking for direction but about being still before God, listening for His voice, and allowing Him to shape our desires to match His. It is a powerful tool that can bring clarity, peace, and confidence in our leadership decisions.

Leading from a place of prayer means we are not relying on our strength but moving in the power and wisdom that come from God.

Through prayer, we find the courage to step out in faith, even when the path ahead is unclear. As you lead, let prayer be the heartbeat of your decisions, actions, and vision casting.

## Clarity and Simplicity in Vision

*A vision statement should be clear, concise, and easily understood by everyone involved.*

A vision statement should be clear, concise, and easily understood by everyone involved. Habakkuk 2:2 instructs us to write the vision plainly so that it can be communicated effectively. Clarity and simplicity are vital to ensuring your vision is accessible and actionable. When your vision is straightforward, it cuts through the noise and distractions, allowing you and those you lead to focus on what truly matters.

A clear and straightforward vision becomes a powerful tool that inspires and mobilizes others. It enables your team, partners, and followers to see their role in the bigger picture and move forward with unity and purpose. As a leader, your ability to communicate your vision clearly will determine how effectively you can rally others to join you in achieving it.

## Aligning Your Vision with God's Will

As Christian women leaders, our vision must align with God's will for our lives and leadership. This alignment requires intentionality, prayer, and a deep reliance on God's wisdom. When your vision is rooted in God's purpose, you can confidently lead, knowing He will bless your efforts and guide your steps, empowering you to inspire and motivate others.

Maintaining a long-term perspective is crucial when casting a vision. Authentic leadership isn't about seeking immediate success but being intentional with each step, trusting that God is directing your path. Your vision should encompass both short-term and long-term goals, guiding your decisions for years to come and instilling a sense of patience and steadfastness in you.

## Crafting a Strategic Plan Rooted in Faith

Once your vision is clear, the next step is to develop a strategic plan that aligns with that vision. A strategic plan provides the roadmap to achieve your goals, offering structure and direction. However, Christians must remember that God should ultimately guide our plans. Proverbs 16:9 reminds us, *"The heart of man plans his way, but the Lord establishes his steps."*

Seek God's guidance throughout the planning process, and be prepared to adjust your plan as He directs. This openness to God's leading ensures that your efforts are aligned with His will and purpose. Trusting in His timing, even when it differs from your own, is vital to walking in obedience and experiencing His blessings.

## Trusting God's Timing and Letting Go

Leadership often involves waiting—waiting on God's timing, His provision, and His direction. Trusting in God's perfect timing requires patience, faith, and a willingness to let go of our agendas. Sometimes, God uses seasons of waiting to mold our character and prepare us for what lies ahead. James 1:2-4 reminds us to count it all joy when we face trials because they produce steadfastness in us.

In these moments of waiting, stand firm in your devotion to the Lord. Trust that He is working behind the scenes, preparing you for the next step in your leadership journey. Let go of any goals or plans that do not align with His will, and embrace the freedom that comes from walking in His purpose.

## Humility and Obedience in Leadership

Authentic leadership is not about striving for strength but humbly surrendering our desires, ambitions, and plans to God. Humility helps us recognize that our wisdom and strength come from the Lord. In our weakness, His power is perfect. In our humility, we become vessels through which His will can be accomplished.

Obedience to God's call, even when it seems counterintuitive or uncomfortable, is where true success lies. As you lead, walk in humility, prayer, and obedience, knowing that God is using you to fulfill a unique purpose that only you can accomplish.

## Taking Action with Accountability

Once you have set your goals, outline specific steps to help you achieve them. These steps should be detailed, actionable, and aligned with your vision. Establish a timeline for each goal and action step and regularly review your progress. Accountability ensures that you stay committed and on track to reach your goals, whether through mentors, partners, or groups.

Identify the resources you need to achieve your goals, including financial, human, and time resources. Pray for God's provision, asking Him to give you divine strategies for acquiring what you need. Trust that as you step out in faith, God will provide everything necessary to fulfill His mission for you.

## Empowering Others Through Your Leadership

As a Christian woman leader, your influence extends far beyond your accomplishments. Your leadership is an opportunity to empower others, lift them up, and help them discover their God-given potential. By standing up and leading with vision, clarity, and faith, you become a beacon of hope and inspiration, guiding others toward the fullness of life that God has for them.

> *As a Christian woman leader, your influence extends far beyond your accomplishments.*

Remember, your leadership is about reaching your goals and empowering those around you to reach theirs. Lead knowing that God has called you to make a difference, and let that calling drive you to stand up, speak out, and lead with courage and conviction.

# APPLICATION QUESTIONS

How does your current leadership vision align with God's purpose for your life? What steps can you take to ensure your vision remains rooted in God's will as you grow?

................................................................................................

................................................................................................

................................................................................................

................................................................................................

................................................................................................

Are there areas in your vision or strategy that need further clarification to avoid confusion or misalignment?

................................................................................................

................................................................................................

................................................................................................

................................................................................................

................................................................................................

How effective are your current processes in supporting your vision and strategic goals? Are there any processes that need updating or replacing? What steps can you take to streamline your processes to align them with your vision and purpose?

..................................................................................................

..................................................................................................

..................................................................................................

..................................................................................................

..................................................................................................

Are you open to adjusting your plans as God directs, even if it means letting go of your desires or preconceived notions? What areas of your strategy might need more flexibility to allow for God's leading?

..................................................................................................

..................................................................................................

..................................................................................................

..................................................................................................

..................................................................................................

# PRAYER

*Heavenly Father,*

*I love you and am so thankful that you know me, see me, and have a vision for my life to make a difference in the world. Surround me with wise advisors to guide, direct, and hold me accountable. Lord, I give you my leadership journey, knowing you will provide me with divine strategies and vision as you guide me and lead me all the days of my life.*

*In Jesus' name, we pray. Amen.*

# ACTIVITY

## CREATE A VISION BOARD
### That Represents Your Business Goals and Spiritual Mission

At the Spark Bold Business retreat, we created vision boards, and the ladies really enjoyed the activity. It helped them gain wisdom and clarity about their business and provided direction for the upcoming year.

Creating a vision board is a powerful way to visually represent your business goals, personal aspirations, and spiritual mission. It serves as a tangible reminder of the vision God has given you and the goals you are working towards. This activity will guide you through the process of creating a vision board that reflects both your business aspirations and your commitment to aligning your life, leadership, and work with God's purpose.

**Materials Needed:**

- ✦ A large poster board, art or cork board
- ✦ Magazines, newspapers, stickers or printed images
- ✦ Scissors
- ✦ Glue or push pins
- ✦ Markers or pens
- ✦ Inspirational quotes, Bible verses, or personal affirmations

# Step-by-Step Guide for Vision Board Activity

## Pray for Guidance

Before you begin crafting your vision board, take time to pray and seek God's guidance. Ask Him to reveal His purpose for your business and to guide you as you set your goals. This step is crucial, as it ensures that your vision board will be aligned with God's will for your life and business.

## Reflect on Your Vision

Spend some time reflecting on the vision you have for your business. What is the purpose of your business? How do you want to impact your customers, community, and the world? Write down your thoughts and ideas, and use them as a foundation for your vision board.

## Set Clear Goals

Based on your reflection, set clear and specific business goals. These goals should be aligned with your vision and purpose. Consider both short-term and long-term goals, and write them down. They will serve as a guide for the images and words you choose for your vision board.

## Gather Images and Words

Look through magazines, newspapers, or online resources for images and words that resonate with your vision and goals. These could include pictures of what you want to achieve, symbols that represent your values, or words and phrases that inspire you. Cut out or print these images and words.

## Include Scripture and Inspirational Quotes

Incorporate Bible verses, inspirational quotes, or personal affirmations that reflect your faith and commitment to aligning your business with God's purpose. These will serve as spiritual anchors for your vision board, reminding you to seek God's guidance in all you do.

## Arrange and Create

Begin arranging the images, words, and Scriptures on your board. There is no right or wrong way to do this—let your creativity flow. As you arrange your board, think about how each element represents your vision and goals. Once you are satisfied with the arrangement, glue or pin everything in place.

## Pray Over Your Vision Board

Once your vision board is complete, take time to pray over it. Ask God to bless your vision and goals and to guide you as you work towards them. Surrender your plans to Him, trusting that He will lead you in the right direction.

## Display Your Vision Board

Place your vision board in a location where you will see it regularly, such as your office, workspace, or bedroom. Use it as a daily reminder of the vision and goals God has given you and your commitment to aligning your business with His purpose.

## Review and Adjust

As you continue on your business journey, regularly review your vision board. Reflect on the progress you have made towards your goals, and make adjustments as needed. Remember that God may lead you in new directions; it is important to remain flexible and open to His guidance.

## Reflection on the Activity

Creating a vision board is not merely about setting goals, it's about aligning those goals with God's purpose and continually seeking His guidance as you work towards them. As you look at your vision board each day, let it be a reminder to pray, seek God's wisdom, and trust in His plan for your life and business. Whether you achieve your goals exactly as planned or find that God has different plans for you, know that you are walking in obedience and faith. That is the true measure of success.

Vision and strategy are essential components of a successful business, but for Christian entrepreneurs, these elements take on a deeper significance. As you develop your vision and strategic plan, remember to root them in your faith, aligning your goals with God's purpose for your life and business. By seeking God's guidance, staying flexible to His leading, and trusting His timing, you can build a business that not only achieves success but also honors and glorifies God.

In the end, it is not just about what you accomplish in your business, but how you accomplish it: with integrity, purpose, and a heart that seeks to serve God in all things.

As you move forward, may your vision be clear, your strategy sound, and your trust in God unwavering, knowing that He will guide your steps and bless your endeavors according to His perfect will.

# Servant Leadership And Putting Others First

When God placed the vision of Spark Media in my heart, I knew it wasn't about me—it was about serving others and advancing His kingdom. The core mission and vision of Spark Media were born out of a desire to equip, empower, and elevate Christian communicators. My goal was to provide the tools and resources they need to boldly share their God-given messages with the world and fulfill the Great Commission to take the gospel to the ends of the earth while fostering a community where we can grow, encourage, and inspire one another.

I didn't create a magazine and podcast network to build my own platform either; it was an act of service. It was about solving a problem and filling a need in the marketplace. At the time, no one was really serving Christian podcasters. I recognized a need for Christian podcasters and communicators to have a space to be seen, celebrated, and supported. With that in mind, I stepped out in faith to create something that would shine a light on their work, amplify their voices, and provide practical resources to grow.

Similarly, the Spark Media Magazine was more than just a publication; it was a labor of love, with each issue highlighting stories of faith, innovation, and creativity while showcasing God's incredible work through Christian podcasters. By featuring independent podcasters and creatives often overlooked by the industry at large, the magazine became a source of encouragement and inspiration for many. It was a place for them to have their work published.

Likewise, the Spark Media Collective and Podcast Network was a hub of collaboration and connection. We created it as a place where podcasters could unite as a community, sharing insights, learning from one another, and uplifting each other. My heart has always been to serve. This network allowed me to pour into others, helping them reach new audiences and fulfill the calling God has placed on their lives.

Servant leadership means leading with humility, putting others first, and trusting God to guide every step. When I created the magazine, collective, and podcast network, I wasn't just building platforms but bridges for others to step into their God-given purpose. Watching others grow, thrive, and succeed is one of the greatest joys of my life, and it's a constant reminder that when we lead with a servant's heart, God multiplies the impact far beyond what we could ever imagine.

## Scriptural Foundation

"But Jesus called them to him and said to them, 'You know that those who are considered rulers of the Gentiles lord it over them, and their great ones exercise authority over them. But it shall not be so among you. But whoever would be great among you must be your servant, and whoever would be first among you must be slave of all. For even the Son of Man came not to be served but to serve, and to give his life as a ransom for many.'"

~ **Mark 10:42-45**

"Do nothing from selfish ambition or conceit, but in humility count others more significant than yourselves. Let each of you look not only to his own interests, but also to the interests of others.

~ **Philippians 2:3-4**

"When he had washed their feet and put on his outer garments and resumed his place, he said to them, 'Do you understand what I have done to you? You call me Teacher and Lord, and you are right, for so I am. If I then, your Lord and Teacher, have washed your feet, you also ought to wash one another's feet. For I have given you an example, that you also should do just as I have done to you. Truly, truly, I say to you, a servant is not greater than his master, nor is a messenger greater than the one who sent him. If you know these things, blessed are you if you do them.'"

~ **John 13:12-17**

## Exploring the Concept of Servant Leadership

> *Leadership is often equated with power and authority, but Jesus presents us with a different model: servant leadership.*

Leadership is often equated with power and authority, but Jesus presents us with a different model: servant leadership. Leadership isn't about climbing to the top; rather, it's about lifting others up along the way. The higher you rise, the more opportunities you have to serve, support, and invest in those around you. That's where real impact occurs. By flipping the script on conventional leadership, servant leadership reminds us that our greatness lies not in acquiring power, but in serving and uplifting others.

Think about how Jesus approached leadership. He didn't climb the corporate ladder; he got down and washed others' feet. Real leadership isn't about rising to the top; it's about helping others up. When we put others first and focus on their needs instead of personal gain, we're truly leading like He did.

When Jesus washed His disciples' feet, He didn't just talk about service—He lived it. Jesus washing His disciples' feet provides a perfect picture of how to lead. He didn't merely speak about serving—He rolled up His sleeves, knelt down, and humbly served others. Jesus demonstrated that leadership isn't about commanding respect but rather about how we treat others. We can follow His example by leading with love and humility, treating everyone with kindness, love, and respect.

Jesus showed us that leadership is not about demanding respect but earning it through love and humility. This example inspires us to do the same in our businesses, reflecting Christ's love in every interaction, whether with our employees, clients, or communities.

## The Impact of Servant Leadership

*Jesus showed us that leadership is not about demanding respect but earning it through love and humility.*

When I'm speaking at conferences or mentoring other women, I try to keep a servant leadership perspective as my focus. Speaking and mentoring is not about building my platform or getting more followers but about serving others, lifting them up, and genuinely caring about their growth and success.

Embracing servant leadership shifts our focus from what we can get to what we can give. This change has profound implications for how we lead. When we lead to serve, we build loyalty, inspire trust, and create a culture where people thrive. People want to be seen and heard, and people who feel valued are more engaged and innovative. When we go the extra mile, those around us become loyal advocates. Communities that witness our commitment to service respect and support us. Servant leadership is not just good for the soul; it's good for everyone.

*Embracing servant leadership shifts our focus from what we can get to what we can give.*

Imagine leading a community where every decision is made with others in mind. What if your team knew their leader was as invested in their success as they are? What if your clients could trust that you always have their best interests at heart? This is the power of servant leadership—it transforms not just your business but everyone it touches. Servant leadership is not merely a strategy; it's a way of life. Leading with a servant's heart creates a culture of empathy, respect, and collaboration.

## Resisting the Pressure to Conform

Do you know how we often think leaders need to be these bold, dominant personalities who command attention? While there's nothing wrong with that style, it's only one way to lead. As Christian women, we can lead like Jesus did, with genuine care and humility.

Use your natural strengths. You may be great at listening or have a knack for solving complex problems creatively. My husband is a problem solver, and God has uniquely gifted Him with intelligence and the ability to look at problems from different angles to come up with creative solutions. Leading differently isn't just okay, it's needed. When you put others first and lead compassionately, you create ripples far beyond yourself. And isn't that what we're after?

*Your unique leadership style matters.*

Your unique leadership style matters. You don't need to copy what others are doing. Lead with your God-given strengths. When you are authentic, you inspire others to do the same. You don't have to fit someone else's mold of leadership.

Your authentic style, shaped by your faith, can profoundly impact right where you are. Don't be afraid to lead in your unique style. The world needs leaders who bring diverse perspectives and approaches. By showing up authentically, you honor God and pave the way for others to do the same.

Servant leadership isn't about checking boxes, it's a mindset that puts others first. As you lead with humility and compassion, your influence will grow not by the number of people who serve you but by how many you serve. You can become a beacon of hope and light through servant leadership, honoring God, and serving those He has placed in your care. Embrace this calling to become a force for good in the world.

When I announced my transition from closing Spark Media to taking on my new role at Trilogyworks. I received a lot of positive sentiments from the Spark Media community. One comment posted on the Spark Media social media page really touched me, and it perfectly summarizes my position as a servant leader.

It was a comment left by Allen C. Paul of God and Gigs. He said, "Misty, it may sound dramatic, but you won't know the true impact of Spark until we all see Jesus face to face. Because only then will the full story be told of every soul, minister, and saint who was blessed by the impact of your faithfulness to this specific project. I know of at least 4,000 people who are thankful for your influence everyday—because without your input I never would have had the confidence to take on my morning devotional—which will hit four million downloads in 2025. More than a podcaster, you are a woman of God, a friend, and someone who knows the power of prioritizing obedience and your first ministry as a wife and helpmeet to your husband. That's something I pray more families will notice as you make your transition to God's next assignment. Thank you for welcoming Lia and me into the Spark family and being a beacon of righteousness in a culture that sorely needs it. His Light will only shine brighter as you walk ever closer to His side."

I don't share this to say look at me, see what a great leader I am. Instead, I share it to show this is the kind of impact you can have on others when you serve from a position of vulnerability.

## Leading with Vulnerability

The world tells us leaders need to have it all together. But think about Jesus—he wept openly, asked for help, and showed his humanity, which is what real leadership looks like. When we're honest about our struggles and mistakes, it builds trust. People connect with our vulnerability and authenticity, not our perfection. Leading isn't about having all the answers, it's about growing together and leaning on God's strength. When we're honest about our struggles and don't pretend to have it all figured out, people trust us more and see that it's okay to be real, grow, and lean on God and one another.

*People connect with our vulnerability and authenticity, not our perfection.*

## Credibility Through Imperfection

We often feel pressure to look like we've 'got it all together' as leaders. But people can tell when we're putting on an act. And that creates distance. When we are open about our struggles, it shows our humanity and helps us build trust. When we say, "I messed up" or "I'm not sure what to do here," we're not weakening our leadership—we're strengthening it. It humanizes us and shows we are not leading from a place of superiority but from a shared journey. This kind of leadership encourages others to take ownership and feel empowered to contribute, confident that their leader values honesty and growth over perfection.

## Empowering Others Through Vulnerability

When I stepped back from Spark Media, many people reached out to share how my decisions inspired them or affirmed their sense of God's guidance. Our actions affect others, and when we lead with humility and vulnerability, it encourages them to do the same.

Leading with vulnerability also fosters an environment where others feel empowered to take risks and be honest about their challenges. When a leader demonstrates vulnerability, it sends a clear message: it's okay to be imperfect. This can cultivate a culture where innovation thrives because people are not afraid to fail. They understand that their leader will support them through failures and help them learn from those experiences rather than punishing them for not getting it right the first time.

In this way, vulnerability in leadership isn't just about the leader; it's about setting a tone for the entire team, organization, or community. It allows for an environment where growth is prioritized over appearances, and every member feels valued for who they are, not just what they can do perfectly.

## Reflecting on Vulnerability

As we strive to embody servant leadership, let's reflect on how we can lead with vulnerability. Are we willing to admit when we're wrong, to ask for help, or to share our struggles with those we lead? This isn't about airing every insecurity but about being real and honest in ways that build trust and deepen relationships.

Remember, our ultimate example of leadership, Jesus, didn't shy away from vulnerability. He led with humility, with a heart open to the pain and struggles of others and a willingness to share His own. As we follow His example, we find that in our vulnerability, we discover a strength that brings others closer and directs them to the One, our trustworthy source of power and grace.

## APPLICATION QUESTIONS

In what ways can you embody servant leadership in your current role? Reflect on specific actions you can take to serve others, whether in your business, community, or personal life.

....................................................................................................................

....................................................................................................................

....................................................................................................................

....................................................................................................................

....................................................................................................................

How do you balance the demands of leadership with the call to humility? Consider times when you've struggled to put others first and how you might approach those situations differently in the future.

....................................................................................................................

....................................................................................................................

....................................................................................................................

....................................................................................................................

....................................................................................................................

What does vulnerability in leadership look like for you? Think about areas where you may have hesitated to show weakness or ask for help. How might embracing vulnerability enhance your leadership?

.................................................................................................

.................................................................................................

.................................................................................................

.................................................................................................

.................................................................................................

Who in your life has exemplified servant leadership, and what have you learned from their example? Identify a mentor, colleague, or leader whose service has impacted you, and reflect on how you can incorporate their influence into your leadership.

.................................................................................................

.................................................................................................

.................................................................................................

.................................................................................................

.................................................................................................

# PRAYER

*Heavenly Father,*

*Lord, we love you, and we praise you. We come before You, seeking to lead as Jesus did—with a heart of service, humility, and love. We thank You for the example of servant leadership that He has set before us, showing us that true greatness lies not in being served but in serving others. Grant us the courage to be vulnerable, to admit our weaknesses, and to rely on Your strength in our imperfections.*

*May our leadership reflect Your love in every interaction. Please help us to see the needs of others and prioritize their well-being above our ambitions. Teach us to be leaders who uplift, inspire, and empower those around us.*

*In Jesus' name, we pray. Amen.*

# Notes

# Innovation For Leaders and Entrepreneurs

Innovation is a creative spark that fuels our leadership and entrepreneurship. As Christian leaders and entrepreneurs, we mirror the creativity of our Creator. In partnership with Him, we take bold, faith-filled steps to blaze trails and pioneer paths that glorify God and advance His Kingdom.

> *Innovation is a creative spark that fuels our leadership and entrepreneurship.*

When God calls us to blaze a trail or step into new ventures, it's not just about strategy—it's about trusting Him enough to step into the unknown. I've seen this firsthand in my ministry, where innovation becomes worship when we follow His lead. Whether you are home raising the next generation for Christ, running a business, or leading a ministry, God wants to use your ingenuity to create and lead. He's given you unique ideas and dreams for a reason. Don't be afraid to think differently—your fresh perspective could be exactly what's needed right now.

## Foundational Scriptures

*"Delight yourself in the Lord, and he will give you the desires of your heart."*

~ Psalm 37:4

*"Trust in the Lord with all your heart, and do not lean on your own understanding. In all your ways acknowledge him, and he will make straight your paths."*

~ Proverbs 3:5-6

*"For God gave us a spirit not of fear but of power and love and self-control."*

~ 2 Timothy 1:7

## Embracing the Spirit of Innovation

The call for innovation has never been more urgent. As Christian women leaders, we are not only called to be stewards of what God has entrusted to us but also pioneers and trailblazers, forging new pathways for His glory. Entrepreneurship is a gift from God that showcases His creativity and purpose. It's about taking bold steps of faith and leveraging our God-given talents to make an impact in the world for Christ.

Our entrepreneurial endeavors are acts of worship when done unto the Lord. Innovation isn't just about creating new things—it's about serving Christ excellently in all we do. Innovation begins with wisdom, which comes from God. Through His wisdom, we gain the prudence and discretion necessary to bring forth creative solutions, divine strategies, and ideas.

> *Our entrepreneurial endeavors are acts of worship when done unto the Lord.*

Psalm 37:4 declares, *"Delight yourself in the Lord, and He will give you the desires of your heart."* This verse has served as a guiding principle throughout my journey, especially during moments of uncertainty and change. It reminds me that when we align our hearts with God's will, He shapes our desires to reflect His purpose for our lives.

God has accomplished remarkable things through women committed to His purposes. Consider the lives of women like Christine Caine, Founder of A21 and Propel Women. Christine is a global speaker, author, and activist who established A21, an international anti-human trafficking organization, as well as Propel Women, an initiative that empowers women to realize their purpose, passion, and potential. Shannon Bream is a successful journalist, bestselling author, and anchor of "Fox News @ Night." Her journalism career is defined by her Christian faith, which she shares openly. Then there's Priscilla Shirer, founder of Going Beyond Ministries. Priscilla is an author, speaker, and actress who has inspired millions through her Bible teaching and ministry, combining her entrepreneurial spirit with her passion for God's Word.

These women are prime examples of blending their entrepreneurial skills and creativity to build incredible ministries and careers that glorify God and inspire others. They exemplify the integration of faith in ministry and business, teaching us how entrepreneurship can serve as a powerful platform for advancing God's Kingdom.

## Seeds of Innovation

> *I love seeing how God ignites creativity in each of us.*

I love seeing how God ignites creativity in each of us. He has placed creative sparks and seeds of innovation within all of us. When we partner with Him, we can transform our ideas into realities that advance His Kingdom. Listen, He's not simply providing us with random ideas—He's inviting us to partner with Him to bring something new into the world.

God is always at work doing new things in the lives of those who are submitted to Him. Innovation is the heartbeat of leadership and entrepreneurship. When aligned with God's purpose, it becomes a powerful force for His Kingdom. Through my journey I've learned that innovation isn't simply about having the next big idea. It's about seeing the opportunities God puts before us, especially when others might see roadblocks. Whether starting a business or leading a ministry, He's given you unique insights to solve problems and meet needs.

## Cultivating a Spirit of Innovation

Begin every entrepreneurial endeavor by praying and asking God for wisdom. Just as Solomon sought wisdom to govern, we should seek the Lord's insight to navigate the complexities of leadership and innovation. For example, I often share my journey of seeking God's wisdom when facing a difficult decision affecting my home and career. After spending years in a successful corporate role at a Fortune 2 company, I felt a deep calling to step away from the security of the job to focus on my family. This decision wasn't easy; it involved significant financial and personal sacrifices.

> *Begin every entrepreneurial endeavor by praying and asking God for wisdom.*

I committed to prayer during this time, seeking God's direction for the next steps. I immersed myself in Scripture, mainly focusing on my life verse of Proverbs 3:5-6: *"Trust in the Lord with all your heart, and do not lean on your own understanding. In all your ways acknowledge him, and he will make straight your paths."*

I went through a similar process years later. I felt a strong conviction that God was calling me to write and speak to encourage women to grow in their faith and leadership. Despite the uncertainties and challenges of transitioning to a new field in my mid-forties, I trusted God's wisdom over my understanding. He doesn't need our works; He desires our hearts. He is more interested in having a relationship with us.

Embracing the ministry call on my life led to founding my first podcast, writing an award-winning Bible study, and becoming a voice of encouragement for many women. This decision changed everything for me – professionally and personally. It showed me how powerful it can be to listen to God's leading and say yes to His call.

God constantly challenges us to go deeper with Him as He leads us into new adventures. Now, in my almost-mid-fifties, God is calling me to my next assignment: to become the COO of Trilogyworks, a technology, strategy, and security consulting firm. He will stretch my

> *God constantly challenges us to go deeper with Him as He leads us into new adventures.*

capacity to learn and grow once more to understand the industry and how He wants to use my gifts and talents in new ways to make a broader Kingdom impact.

We must stay attuned to the Lord's leading and be willing to follow where He leads. If you aren't sure what God wants to do next in your life, you need divine intervention or a fresh move of the Holy Spirit. Carve out time to fast, spend time in His Word, and pray. God loves to give us creative new ideas, strategies, and opportunities to align our hearts to His kingdom's purposes.

## Don't be Afraid to Take Calculated Risks

> *God doesn't call us to 'play it safe.'*

Innovation often requires us to step outside our comfort zone and take calculated risks. I've discovered something profound about embracing risks: God doesn't call us to 'play it safe.' At times, we find ourselves trapped in our comfort zone, keeping things small and manageable. Often, we hold ourselves back, playing small because it feels safe, comfortable, and easy. But God didn't create us to live a life confined by fear or uncertainty. He calls us to trust Him, step out in faith, and take bold, calculated risks that align with His will for our lives. When we play small, we limit what God can accomplish through us. We miss out on the miracles He wants to perform, not just for us but through us for the benefit of others.

But here's the truth: when God nudges us to step out, He's already mapped out the path. Don't let fear hold you back from the amazing things He's prepared for you. Trust God as you take risks, knowing He is faithful to guide and protect you. Taking risks is often essential to stepping into the fullness of our God-given purpose.

The Bible is filled with stories of men and women who took incredible risks because they trusted God's promises. Think about David, who faced Goliath with nothing but a sling and a few stones. Or Esther, who risked her life by approaching the king to save her people. These weren't acts of recklessness; they were acts of faith. They didn't play small. They embraced the full measure of their calling, trusting that God would meet them in their moment of need. And He did.

We must remember that taking risks in faith is not about recklessness but about obedience. It's about hearing God's voice, discerning His will, and stepping out even when the path ahead is unclear. The truth is that playing small serves no one. It doesn't serve God, it doesn't serve others, and it certainly doesn't serve you. When you hold back, you're not only withholding your gifts and talents from the world, but you're also diminishing the power of God at work in your life.

Taking risks is an act of worship and a declaration of trust in the One who holds your future. It's acknowledging that God's plans for you are bigger than your fears, more significant than your doubts, and bigger than any obstacle you might face. So don't be afraid to dream big, step out of your comfort zone, and take the risks God calls you to take. Remember, God didn't give you a spirit of fear but of power, love, and a sound mind (2 Timothy 1:7). When you step out in faith, you allow His power to be perfected in your weakness. So, let's commit to not playing small. Let's take the risks that God is calling us to take, knowing He is faithful to lead, guide, and provide every step of the way.

## Evaluate and Adapt

> *God-inspired innovation transforms ordinary ideas into extraordinary Kingdom impact.*

God-inspired innovation transforms ordinary ideas into extraordinary Kingdom impact. Regularly assess your business strategies and be open to change. Innovation is an ongoing process that requires flexibility and a willingness to adapt to new circumstances.

Innovation requires action despite uncertainties. Waiting for perfect conditions can hinder progress, but trusting in God allows us to move forward in faith, sowing seeds that will bear fruit in due season and giving us hope for the future.

In 2020, the world experienced an unprecedented disruption that compelled many of us to rethink our strategies and adapt swiftly. This period served as a powerful reminder that disruption often sparks innovation. When traditional methods of conducting business, hosting events, and engaging with audiences were abruptly overturned, it created opportunities to pivot and explore new paths. Virtual events, digital content, and online communities became the lifeblood of my work, leading to the growth of Spark Media in ways I hadn't previously imagined. This experience reinforced a fundamental truth: innovation flourishes in times of challenge. When the familiar is stripped away, we are driven to think creatively, experiment, and discover new solutions that meet the moment and propel us into uncharted territories.

# APPLICATION QUESTIONS

What areas of your life or business could benefit from a fresh perspective or innovative approach?

........................................................................................................

........................................................................................................

........................................................................................................

........................................................................................................

........................................................................................................

........................................................................................................

How can you intentionally seek God's wisdom in your entrepreneurial endeavors?

........................................................................................................

........................................................................................................

........................................................................................................

........................................................................................................

........................................................................................................

........................................................................................................

What steps can you take this week to cultivate a spirit of innovation in your business or ministry?

..................................................................................................
..................................................................................................
..................................................................................................
..................................................................................................
..................................................................................................
..................................................................................................

Who can you collaborate with within your community to bring new ideas to life?

..................................................................................................
..................................................................................................
..................................................................................................
..................................................................................................
..................................................................................................
..................................................................................................

How can you ensure that your innovations are aligned with God's purpose for your life?

..................................................................................................

..................................................................................................

..................................................................................................

..................................................................................................

..................................................................................................

..................................................................................................

# PRAYER

*Heavenly Father,*

*We thank You for the gift of creativity and innovation that You have placed within each of us. Help us to be wise stewards of these gifts, seeking Your guidance in all our endeavors. We pray for the courage to take bold steps of faith, trusting that You will make a way in the wilderness and create rivers in the desert. May our work glorify You and advance Your Kingdom. Guide us, Lord, as we innovate and create, always for Your glory.*

*In Jesus' name, we pray. Amen.*

# BUILDING A SUPPORTIVE COMMUNITY

As Christian women called to lead, we thrive best when we walk alongside others who share our faith and values. The journey of leadership isn't meant to be solitary or lonely. However, sometimes, it can feel lonely as God sets us apart and anoints us for the work He's called us to do. The truth is that the higher you climb, the fewer people can go with you.

Y'all, I can't tell you how many times I've seen the power of doing life together as believers. That first taste of a genuine Christian community changed everything for me. Our young married Sunday school class wasn't just a weekly meet-up. It became our second family. We'd meet at our leader's home for lunch-and-learns, trading stories about our struggles and victories as newlyweds with young children. We would gather for lunch, Bible study, park days, birthdays, baby showers, and game nights. Our intimacy in friendship allowed us to get honest about our marriage challenges and learn to pray for each other.

The memories still make me smile—watching our children run and play in the park, celebrating each precious baby shower like our own, and those legendary game nights or birthday dinners that had us laughing until late in the evening. But it was more than just fun times, and these weren't just church friends. They were the people who loved, prayed, and carried us through life's highest highs and lowest lows.

Looking back, I realize God was teaching us what it meant to walk in Christian fellowship to "do life together"—bearing one another's burdens, celebrating each victory, and growing deeper in our faith as we studied His Word, read life-changing books and applied it to our daily lives. Our little Sunday school class laid the foundation for how I understand Christian community even today. It's a reminder of the importance of staying committed to building relationships, even when it's not easy.

Do you know that verse in Proverbs about iron sharpening iron? It's so true! When I gather with my sisters in Christ, something beautiful happens—we grow stronger together, challenge each other, and become better versions of ourselves. And don't get me started on what Solomon said in Ecclesiastes about two being better than one. I've experienced that truth! There have been countless moments when I needed someone to lift me up, dust me off, and remind me of God's promises. That's why I'm passionate about building an authentic community. The growth and transformation from serving one another are truly inspiring.

## Scriptural Foundation

*"Iron sharpens iron, and one man sharpens another."*

**~ Proverbs 27:17**

*"Two are better than one because they have a good reward for their toil. For if they fall, one will lift up his fellow. But woe to him who is alone when he falls and has not another to lift him up!"*

**~ Ecclesiastes 4:9-10**

*"Not neglecting to meet together, as is the habit of some, but encouraging one another, and all the more as you see the Day drawing near."*

**~ Hebrews 10:25**

## Mastermind Journey

Fast forward to when I first began my writing journey in 2016. I knew it would be necessary to surround myself with others who shared the same passion and drive to write and speak for Jesus. When I got home from attending She Speaks, a conference for Christian communicators hosted by Proverbs 31 Ministries, a few friends gathered in my home every month to encourage and inspire one another in our calling. These masterminds went from four passionate women to a thriving community of authors, speakers, podcasters, entrepreneurs, and leaders.

God used that little group to shape me. We would get together each week, spilling our hearts about what we were learning. We would meet regularly and share training, inspiration, goals, challenges, and victories, all while encouraging one another to pursue the calling of God in our lives. This small but influential community became a source of inspiration and accountability. Even my children recognized how extraordinary these gatherings were. One day, my youngest son exclaimed, "Your mastermind meeting is one of the neatest things you do, Mom." In those early gatherings, I witnessed the transformative power of community—a power that would later inspire the creation of the Spark Collective.

Community was at the very heart of everything we did at Spark Media. When I founded Spark Media, I was convinced that we were not meant to walk this journey alone, especially in the fast-paced, often isolating world of media and content creation. God calls us to gather, support, and uplift one another. The Spark Collective was born out of this desire to create a vibrant, Christ-centered community where podcasters, creators, and leaders could connect, grow, and thrive together.

The Spark Collective became more than just a group of podcasters; it became a family of believers who shared a passion for using media to spread the Gospel and make a difference in the world. We came together online to learn, encourage, and push one another to new heights, always keeping Christ at the center of our work. This community was a place where ideas flourished, collaborations happened, and dreams turned into reality—all within the safety and support of beautiful friendships and community.

## Collaboration with Others is Key

I love the phrase 'collaboration over competition.' When you stop seeing other Christian women as competition and start seeing them as collaborators, your entire world will open up! This beautiful thing happens when we lay down our measuring sticks and pick up each other's dreams instead. It is difficult for God to bless us if we are tight-fisted with our dreams and plans. The Kingdom of God isn't a pie where we must fight for our slice.

When we lock arms and uplift each other, there's more than enough to go around! I love what happens when we trade comparison for collaboration—it's like watching God multiply our loaves and fishes. Some of my biggest breakthroughs came when I built ladders for others to succeed. Let this truth sink in: your success isn't my failure, and my win isn't your loss. We're better together, doing life side-by-side, cheering each other on. Remember this: Lighting another candle doesn't lose its flame; it just makes the room brighter. So come on, sister, let's shine together!

*your success isn't my failure, and my win isn't your loss.*

Let me tell you what happens when passionate believers unite in a common purpose—it is life-changing! I've seen some of the most amazing ideas bloom, bouncing ideas and thoughts off each other and dreaming together. Whether you attend a conference or retreat, or grab coffee or lunch with friends, there is something special about spending time with other believers who get your vision and add their spark to it.

Innovation and collaboration thrive in a community. Some of my closest business partnerships started with a simple "Hey, what if we…"

over lunch. And now? Those casual chats have turned into Kingdom-building ventures I never could have imagined. When you find your tribe of people who love Jesus and love what they do, magic happens. They'll see things in your ideas that you missed, cheer you on when you doubt yourself, and jump in to help make it happen. When we plug into a thriving community, we surround ourselves with others who will inspire us and offer fresh perspectives, encouragement, and support. Each discussion sparks innovative ideas, and collaborative projects create opportunities to share insights and forge meaningful partnerships.

*Innovation and collaboration thrive in a community.*

Y'all, when I look back on this wild journey of starting Spark Media, writing books, speaking, and jumping into the podcast world, I can tell you three things that have been absolute game-changers for me: being resilient and getting back up when life knocks you down, staying hungry to learn, and building relationships with other dreamers.

Let me be real with you. This path hasn't been all sunshine and roses. Building Spark Media? Whew! There were days I wanted to throw in the towel. But here's what I learned: Every roadblock was redirecting me to God's better "yes."

Listen, if you're starting out, I want you to know something. Those setbacks you experience are part of the story. Every single one of them taught me something I needed to know. Don't let them scare you off! Some of my biggest breakthroughs came right after my worst failures. And please, please find your people, those precious souls who'll pray with you, cry with you, and believe in your dream even when you don't. I wouldn't be here today without my community pushing me forward when I wanted to quit. Please don't shy away from obstacles; see them as stepping stones toward your next breakthrough. Surround yourself with a collaborative community that uplifts you, and remember, every outstanding achievement is a testament to unwavering persistence.

Networking and collaboration have played an equally vital role in widening my circle and growing my influence. Remember, the relationships you cultivate today can unlock future opportunities you never imagined possible. In the early stages of your journey, intentionally seek connections with those who share your vision and passion by attending industry events, engaging in online communities and meaningful conversations.

Networking isn't just about exchanging contact information; it's about nurturing relationships that lead to mutual growth and unlock new possibilities. Proverbs 27:17 teaches, *"Iron sharpens iron, and one man sharpens another."*

Embracing a growth mindset fuels your relevance and innovation. The media landscape and technology are evolving at lightning speed, making continuous learning and growing imperative. Dedicating time to mastering new skills, staying abreast of industry trends, and exploring emerging technologies can enhance your work. When I first began writing, blogging, speaking, and podcasting, I regularly attended conferences and industry events. I dedicated time to learning through online courses and in-person events. My self-study broadened my knowledge and helped me better understand best practices and industry trends. The

> *Embracing a growth mindset fuels your relevance and innovation.*

more you learn, the more valuable you become to the community you serve.

## The Power of Connection

We are called not only to lead but to nurture and build communities that reflect the love and grace of Christ. A supportive community is more than just a network—it's a family of believers who uplift, encourage, and walk alongside one another in faith and purpose.

In community, you will find a sense of belonging and a deep sense of value, which is essential for your leadership journey. Ecclesiastes 4:9-10 highlights the importance of community for practical support and the spiritual and emotional sustenance that comes from walking in fellowship with others.

## The Importance of a Supportive Community

*Isolation is a common trap in leadership.*

Isolation is a common trap in leadership. The demands and pressures can lead us to believe we must carry the burden alone. But, ya'll, God designed us for community! A supportive community provides a safe space for learning and growth while holding us accountable. In this sharpening process, we become better leaders and more effective in our God-given missions. Surrounding ourselves with a supportive community is not just beneficial; it is essential for growth and leadership development.

## Practical Tips for Building a Supportive Community

Pray for God's guidance. One of the first steps in building a supportive community is to seek God's wisdom. He knows exactly who we need in our circle, so ask Him to bring the women to you who will encourage, challenge, and support you in your calling. Then, trust that He will place the right individuals in your path at the proper time to help you lead, grow, and thrive.

Building a community requires intention. Connect with others regularly, plan lunches and coffee dates, or send encouraging notes. Intentionality means actively pursuing relationships and a community that encourage, challenge, and uplift you. Being intentional involves purposefully engaging with others—showing up, being present, and investing in those around you. Consistently attending church events, joining Bible studies, and creating small groups of like-minded women have inspired my leadership journey.

Consistent and intentional interaction is vital to forming meaningful relationships with others who can encourage and inspire us. For a community to be genuinely supportive, it must be built on trust. Be open and transparent about your struggles, victories, and goals. Encourage others to do the same. Vulnerability invites connection and fosters a deeper level of support. So, don't just wait for community to happen; be intentional about building and nurturing it, knowing that it's vital to fulfilling the purpose God has placed on your life.

## Serve One Another

A supportive community thrives on mutual service. Look for ways to serve those in your community – whether through prayer, acts of kindness, offering wisdom, or simply being a listening ear. As you pour into others, you'll find that your needs are often met. Serving one another in a community is at the heart of living out our faith and fulfilling our God-given purpose.

> **When we choose to serve others, we reflect Christ's love.**

When we choose to serve others, we reflect Christ's love. Serving isn't just about meeting needs; it's also about seeing others through the eyes of Jesus and valuing their worth. When we invest our time, talents, resources, and energy into others, we are uplifted too.

To create a thriving community, serve one another, and make an environment where your sisters can be encouraged, uplifted, and empowered to step into their callings. Serving is a way of life reflecting Christ's heart and transforming our communities. By prioritizing service, we cultivate a spirit of unity and love that not only blesses others but also deepens our walk with God.

## Celebrate Each Other's Successes

It is essential to celebrate the successes of those around us. A vibrant community lifts each other up and celebrates wins together. My heart overflows with joy thinking about how the Spark Media Awards illuminated and elevated the voices of Christian podcasters. At our Spark Media Award ceremonies, I watched Christian podcasters light up as they were recognized for their dedication and impact. When we gathered to celebrate at our ceremonies, I witnessed firsthand how recognition can breathe fresh wind into others. The smiles, tears, hugs, and testimonies shared at our ceremonies reveal how meaningful it is to have your work acknowledged by your peers.

The friendships formed and encouragement shared at these award ceremonies rippled out far beyond our celebrations. These awards became more than just trophies. Our celebrations were milestones marking renewed purpose. Seeing nominees encourage one another and form lasting friendships was an incredible honor. It was a great reminder that we weren't just building platforms; we were building a community, spurring each other toward excellence.

It's important to remember that we are not in competition with one another. By celebrating the accomplishments of others, we affirm their gifts and calling and give them hope to press on when the journey is difficult. We can all flourish by fostering an environment where everyone feels seen, valued, and supported. Let's be intentional about lifting each other up, celebrating milestones both big and small, and watching how God uses our collective victories to inspire and propel us all forward in our callings.

## Stay Committed

Building a supportive community takes time and effort. So, we need to stay committed to the process even when it feels challenging. Remember that relationships are long-term investments yielding spiritual and emotional rewards. The journey is better when we walk it together, supporting and uplifting one another every step of the way.

*Building a supportive community takes time and effort.*

## The Biblical Model of Community

The early church serves as a powerful example of a supportive community. Acts 2:42 describes this community: *"And they devoted themselves to the apostles' teaching and the fellowship, to the breaking of bread and the prayers."* This Scripture reflects the core elements of a Christ-centered community: teaching, fellowship, shared meals, and prayer.

As Christian women leaders, we can draw inspiration from the early church and strive to build communities equally devoted to these practices. By grounding our communities in Scripture, prayer, and genuine fellowship, we create an environment where each member can thrive and fulfill their God-given potential. This biblical model of community, as seen in the early church, serves as a powerful guide for us in building and nurturing our supportive communities.

## A Call to Action

Building a supportive community is not just a leadership strategy; it's a spiritual mandate. As you continue in your leadership journey, I encourage you to invest in the relationships around you. Seek out those who will support and sharpen you and be that support for others. My friends and I uplift each other by sharing encouraging or funny words through Instagram, Scriptures from our quiet times that resonate with us, and books that inspire our hearts.

Let's commit to creating spaces where other women can grow in faith and confidently step into leadership roles to fulfill God's unique calling. We can build a supportive community that shines brightly for the Kingdom of God.

# APPLICATION QUESTIONS

How has being part of a community impacted your leadership journey so far? Reflect on specific instances where others have supported or encouraged you as a leader.

..................................................................................................

..................................................................................................

..................................................................................................

..................................................................................................

..................................................................................................

How can you be more intentional about building and nurturing relationships within your community? Consider what steps you can take to connect more deeply with those around you.

..................................................................................................

..................................................................................................

..................................................................................................

..................................................................................................

..................................................................................................

Think about a time when you served someone in your community. How did that experience impact you, and how did it contribute to building a stronger connection?

..................................................................................................
..................................................................................................
..................................................................................................
..................................................................................................
..................................................................................................

What steps can you take to celebrate the successes of others in your community more effectively? How can this practice strengthen your relationships and the overall community?

..................................................................................................
..................................................................................................
..................................................................................................
..................................................................................................
..................................................................................................

# PRAYER

*Heavenly Father,*

*We come before You with hearts full of gratitude for the communities You have placed in our lives. Thank You for the gift of fellowship, for the brothers and sisters in Christ who walk alongside us in our leadership journey. Lord, we ask for Your guidance as we seek to build and nurture supportive communities that reflect Your love and grace. Help us to be intentional in our relationships, to serve one another with joy, and to celebrate the successes You bring into our lives.*

*Father, we pray our communities will be rooted in Your Word, grounded in prayer, and strengthened by the bonds of trust and openness. May we be instruments of Your peace, offering encouragement and support to those around us. Teach us to sharpen one another as iron sharpens iron and to lift each other when we fall.*

*Lord, we ask that You continue to bring the right people into our lives—those who will challenge us, inspire us, and help us grow closer to You. Let our communities be places where dreams are nurtured, ideas flourish, and Your Kingdom's work is advanced.*

*In Jesus' name, we pray. Amen.*

# Notes

# EMBRACING GOD'S DIRECTION IN SEASONS OF TRANSITION

Life transitions often arrive uninvited, wreaking havoc on our best-laid plans and leaving us with more questions than answers. Whether it's a child leaving for college, the sudden loss of a loved one, a career shift, or an empty nest, these moments can shake our identity and purpose. Often, we don't realize how much of who we are is wrapped up in these roles.

Yet, within the upheaval lies an opportunity to realign with God's purpose for our lives and what He has for us in the next season. While transitions may be disorienting and sometimes even painful, they are fertile grounds for growth and renewal. For me, 2024 was a year of quiet quitting, pruning, cutting back, and laying down my way of doing things to embrace God's new plan for my life. It was a year of transition, change, and walking through open doors.

In seasons of change, God keeps bringing me back to His unchanging truth. When everything around me shifts like sand, I cling to the

> *In seasons of change, God keeps bringing me back to His unchanging truth.*

promises He's written on my heart. Some days, the journey forward feels like taking tiny steps in the dark, but His gentle whisper guides me through. Each time I walk through uncertainty, I see more clearly how He writes stories that are far more beautiful than anything I could plan. My heart has learned to rest, knowing that even when I can't see the path ahead, He's already there, working out every detail with tender care.

## Foundational Scripture

*"Seek first the kingdom of God and his righteousness, and all these things will be added to you."*

~ Matthew 6:33

*"When you pass through the waters, I will be with you; and through the rivers, they shall not overwhelm you."*

~ Isaiah 43:2

*"I can do all things through him who strengthens me."*

~ Philippians 4:13

**Life can change at a moment's notice.**

Life can change at a moment's notice. Your kids go off to school, you move to a new location, lose your job, suddenly become a window, or have an empty nest. The sudden change has a way of shaking us to our core, unraveling the carefully woven plans we've held onto so tightly. It often arrives unannounced, like a storm that sweeps through on a clear day, leaving us to pick up the pieces. But there's an opportunity to see life through a new lens during the chaos and uncertainty. Sudden change forces us to confront what truly matters, adapt, grow, and trust in a plan greater than our own.

## Broken Arms: An Unexpected Detour

My life took a sudden detour the day I was out for a ride with my boys when I broke both of my arms in a bicycling accident. One moment, I was cruising down the trail, and the next, I was catapulted over the handlebars, crashing onto the concrete. Unable to move, I lay there in the middle of the woods, helplessly waiting for the paramedics. Unsure of the extent of my injuries, I forced myself to remain still, focusing on each breath, trying to stay calm. After what felt like an eternity, the paramedics arrived and rushed me to the hospital.

As I lay in the hospital bed with casts on both arms, reality hit me like a tidal wave. How was I going to care for my family? How could I manage even the simplest of tasks for myself? I was overwhelmed with questions and doubts, feeling utterly powerless. But in that place of vulnerability, I discovered a strength I never knew I had. Each challenge, whether trying to eat, brush my teeth, wash my face, or care for myself, forced me to lean on God more than ever. It wasn't just about surviving the day; it was about trusting Him with every detail, every moment. This experience taught me that true strength is found in vulnerability, and it's okay to lean on God and others for support.

Those months were some of the hardest I've ever endured and some of the most transformative in my life. My family rallied around me, and I learned the power of surrender. Being stripped of my independence made me see life through an entirely different lens. I realized that while I couldn't control what happened to me, I could control my response. The experience of breaking my arms and going through the healing process taught me that surrender is not a sign of weakness but a powerful tool for transformation. We can truly grow and change in our moments of surrender.

> *We can truly grow and change in our moments of surrender.*

During this time, I also discovered a great sense of humility and a deeper faith that would carry me through the physical healing and emotional and spiritual growth that followed. What began as a painful accident became a defining moment in my life, reminding me that God's strength is made perfect in our weakness. During those times when I couldn't do anything for myself, God showed me how deeply He loves me—not because of anything I could do for Him, but simply because I am His daughter. And do you know what, friend? He wants you to know that you are loved by Him, too, and nothing can separate you from His love. Our identity stems from who we are, not what we do. This season of surrender gave me a new appreciation for the mundane, helped me cultivate what matters most, and prepared me for my next chapter.

## Prioritizing What Matters Most

> *The key to cultivating what matters and redeeming our time begins with prioritization.*

The key to cultivating what matters and redeeming our time begins with prioritization. Not everything on your to-do list carries the same weight, and not every opportunity that comes our way is meant to be pursued. It takes wisdom and an awareness of the Holy Spirit to understand what we should seek and what we should not. As a leader, it's crucial for us to discern what God is calling us to focus on in each season of life. By prioritizing what truly matters, we can direct our energy and attention toward what will bring us closer to God and fulfill our purpose.

Matthew 6:33 reminds us to *"Seek first the kingdom of God and his righteousness, and all these things will be added to you."* This means that our priority should always be our relationship with God. When we start our day with Him through prayer, reading Scripture, and seeking His guidance, we align our hearts with His will, which helps us make better decisions about how to spend our time.

After consulting God, consider the other areas of your life that require your attention. Your family, work, ministry, and personal well-being are all important, but they may need to be prioritized differently depending on your season. Take time to evaluate what truly matters and be willing to say no to things that don't align with your purpose and priorities.

## Navigating Transitions

As women, we often navigate seasons and transitions that can leave us uncertain and directionless. I felt deeply uncertain when our firstborn son went to kindergarten. This marked a significant transition for our family. I worked full time but longed to be home raising my boys.

We all must navigate transitions at some point in our lives. Whether it's sending our children off to school, facing an empty nest, enduring the pain of divorce, or experiencing the deep sorrow of widowhood, these seasons can shake the very foundation of our lives. Yet, in these moments, we must remember that we are never alone. God's reassuring presence is with us, guiding us through and preventing us from being overwhelmed.

Yet, in these moments of transition, God calls us closer to Him, urging us to embrace His guidance and discover our purpose anew. These seasons are not the end of our story but the beginning of a new chapter written by the Author of our faith.

## Finding Direction in God's Plan

*During seasons of transition, it's common to feel lost and directionless.*

During seasons of transition, it's common to feel lost and directionless. The roles we once held—whether as mothers, wives, daughters, sisters, or caretakers—may no longer occupy the same space in our lives. This can leave us questioning our purpose and wondering where to go next.

God's direction often begins where our understanding ends. Seasons of transition are opportunities to rediscover your purpose and who God has called you to be. They are also a time to explore new passions, develop new skills, and step into roles you may have never imagined. You'll find a renewed sense of purpose and direction by seeking His will and allowing Him to guide you.

## Facing Uncertainty with Faith

Transitions often come with a range of emotions, from grief and sadness to uncertainty and fear. It's natural to feel a sense of loss when moving from one season of life to another. As a Christian woman, you might feel the weight of these emotions more deeply, knowing that God has a plan but struggling to see it in the moment. This can lead to a period of soul-searching where you lean on God more than ever.

I know this to be true because it has happened to me repeatedly in my life.

Life's big changes have swept through my world many times, bringing waves of sadness and many questions. I've spent countless hours in prayer, tears flowing, asking God to reveal His path when everything felt murky and uncertain.

The times when familiar routines slip away can leave such an ache in your heart. Yet every single time, even when I couldn't see past my tears, God was weaving together a beautiful tapestry. Pruning can be painful. Looking back at my garden, I can't help but think about how pruning works—those cuts appear so harsh at first. The leaves and branches fall away; it seems like such waste. But that is precisely what God has done in my life through these transitions. He has carefully trimmed away what needed to go, making space for new growth I never could have imagined. Each uncertain season has drawn me closer to Him, teaching me to trust His gentle hands even when I don't understand His methods.

Friend, I know uncertainty can be overwhelming. When life as we know it changes, it's natural to feel lost. The familiar routines and roles that once defined our days are suddenly gone, leaving a void that can seem impossible to fill. But it's important to remember that even in the midst of uncertainty, God is always with us. He sees the bigger picture and has a good plan for us, even when we can't see it ourselves.

In these times of transition, draw close to God and seek His guidance and comfort. These moments of change can become pivotal in your spiritual journey as you rely on your faith and trust in God's plan. Transitions can also be a time of pruning, where God removes things from your life to prepare you for new growth and opportunities. I've certainly felt this pruning, and as a gardener, I know that pruning, while painful, produces good fruit.

## Trusting God's Plan in Transitions

*Uncertainty is not a detour; it's an invitation to trust God's perfect plan,*

Uncertainty is not a detour; it's an invitation to trust God's perfect plan, a hopeful perspective to adopt during times of change. Instead of dwelling on what we've lost, we can shift our mindset to what God may be preparing us for. This is a time to lean into God's word, seek His guidance in prayer by asking specific questions about the future, and trust that He is leading us toward something new and beautiful. His plan is filled with hope; even amid confusion, we can remain optimistic about the future He has in store for us.

Feeling lost is a profoundly unsettling experience. It's as if the world around you continues to move forward, yet you're stuck in place, unsure where to turn or how to move forward. The roles and responsibilities that once gave your life structure and meaning may have shifted or disappeared altogether, leaving you with a sense of emptiness. You might wake up each day feeling a heavy cloud of confusion and a lack of direction, wondering what your next steps should be and questioning whether you even have the strength to take them.

Trusting God's timing and plan means being patient when things don't go as planned, being open to His redirection, and having faith that He is working all things together for good. It also means letting go of the need to control every aspect of your schedule and allowing

God to lead you. This can be difficult if you are a control freak like me, but there is peace in letting go and trusting God.

## Finding Purpose When You Feel Lost

Transitions in life often force you to re-evaluate your identity and purpose. As roles and responsibilities shift, you may struggle with feelings of inadequacy or a lack of direction. This is an opportunity to rediscover who you are in Christ and to seek His will for the new season ahead. It's a time to remember that your identity is not rooted in your roles but in your relationship with God.

> *Transitions in life often force you to re-evaluate your identity and purpose.*

These feelings of being lost can lead to a profound sense of purposelessness. When the things that once defined your identity—being a mother, a wife, or a caregiver—are no longer present in the same way, it's easy to feel like a ship adrift without a compass. You might find yourself asking, "What now?" The future can seem like a vast, intimidating unknown, and the passions that once fueled your life may feel distant or even extinguished.

But in these moments of uncertainty and confusion, God is not distant. He is closer than ever, waiting to guide you through the fog of uncertainty and into a renewed sense of purpose. God understands your pain and confusion and offers a path forward, even when you can't see it yourself. Scripture reminds us, *"The Lord is near to the brokenhearted and saves the crushed in spirit"* (Psalm 34:18), a powerful promise that assures us of His constant support. Remember, you are never alone in your journey of faith.

## Passion and Purpose

*Reigniting your passion is the fuel that powers your purpose.*

Reigniting your passion is the fuel that powers your purpose. But how do we sustain that passion, especially during challenging seasons when everything feels like an uphill battle? First, we must stay connected to our why. Regularly reminding yourself of why you started this journey, the calling you felt deep within, and the impact you're striving to make can make a huge difference. Surround yourself with a community of people to encourage and uplift you who remind you of your purpose when the passion wanes. Finally, make sure to practice self-care along the way. Resting, recharging, and renewing your spirit is crucial for sustaining the fire that drives you. So make sure to reward yourself and celebrate the milestones along the way.

God has a unique purpose for you, even in this new season. He created you with a specific design, and His plans for you didn't end when your circumstances changed. These words are not just for others; they are for you right now, in this season of feeling lost. God's plans for you are filled with hope and purpose, and He will reveal them to you as you seek Him. You are not just a part of His plan, you are the focus of His plan. He values you more than you can imagine.

As you turn to God, He renews your passion and ignites a new fire within you. What may seem like the end of one chapter is, in fact, the beginning of another—one where God is calling you to new opportunities, new ministries, and new ways to serve Him. It may take time, and the path may not always seem clear, but God is faithful. He will restore your sense of purpose and lead you to a place where your passions align with His will for your life.

In these moments, prayer becomes a lifeline. By bringing your feelings of being lost and directionless to God, you open your heart to His guidance. The Holy Spirit, our Comforter and Counselor, will gently guide you toward the passions and purposes God has prepared for you. As you spend time in His presence, He will renew your spirit, rekindle your enthusiasm, and help you discover the joy of walking in His will.

Remember that God has not forgotten you, no matter how lost you feel. He is the Good Shepherd who seeks out His lost sheep, bringing them back into the fold and leading them to green pastures. You will find the purpose and passion you've been searching for in Him, and He will guide you into a future filled with His grace and love.

## Gaining Motivation through God's Strength

Motivation can wane during times of change. The emotional toll can drain the energy and enthusiasm that once fueled our days of transition. But we must remember that our strength comes not from our circumstances but from the Lord. The joy of the Lord is our strength, and when our strength fails, God's power prevails.

> *To regain motivation, start taking small steps in faith.*

To regain motivation, start taking small steps in faith. Set aside time each day to be still before the Lord, grab your Bible and journal, and allow His presence to refresh and renew you. Surround yourself with a supportive community of believers who can encourage and uplift you. Most importantly, keep your eyes fixed on Jesus, the source of your strength and the Author of your motivation.

## Stepping into the New with Courage

Courage is a character quality that distinguishes leaders. As you navigate this season of transition, remember that you are not alone. Just as God was with me when I broke my arms, cared for my in-laws both of whom had brain tumors, or when I buried my stillborn son, God is with you too, guiding you into a new chapter filled with possibilities and purpose. While the path may be uncertain, His promises are unwavering and true. He has a plan for your life, a plan filled with hope. Your new beginning is God's continuation of His perfect plan.

The sweetest surprises have come in those seasons when God shifted everything around in my life. Through each change, He's opened my eyes to see my gifts in fresh ways—like when He nudged me toward podcasting after years of being home and doing ministry in other areas. Looking back, I can trace His fingerprints on every transition, showing me new paths I never would have discovered. Those uncertain seasons stretched my faith but taught me to dream bigger and say yes even when my knees shake. Sometimes, serving Him looks different than we imagined, but watching Him weave our gifts into His bigger story brings such deep joy. Every time I've surrendered my plans and followed His lead, He's shown me purposes more meaningful than anything I could have mapped out.

Sweet friend, my heart beats fast thinking about the fresh season God is unfolding in your life. I've walked through enough changes to know they can shake us up and leave us wondering which way to turn. But let me tell you what I've learned in my messy moments of transition. God holds your hand extra tight during these times. He's molding your heart and building muscles of faith you didn't even know you needed.

In my quiet time, I've been reading Joshua's book and pondering how he must have felt stepping into the promised land. With reports of scary giants and complaints from the people, Joshua had the heart to take the land. Like him, we sometimes need that gentle reminder to be strong and courageous and to embrace the unknown. Take that brave step forward, knowing your Father delights in showing you the way. He's writing your story with such tender care. These uncertain days are crafting you into exactly who He created you to be.

> *Take that brave step forward, knowing your Father delights in showing you the way.*

## APPLICATION QUESTIONS

What areas of your life feel uncertain right now? Where is fear holding you back? How can you invite God into those spaces to provide clarity and peace?

...........................................................................................................

...........................................................................................................

...........................................................................................................

...........................................................................................................

...........................................................................................................

As you seek God's guidance in finding your new purpose, what steps can you take to help discover His direction for this season?

...........................................................................................................

...........................................................................................................

...........................................................................................................

...........................................................................................................

...........................................................................................................

When do you feel the most unmotivated? How can you draw on God's strength during those times?

..................................................................................................

..................................................................................................

..................................................................................................

..................................................................................................

..................................................................................................

# PRAYER

*Heavenly Father,*

*You are Lord over all seasons. In my season of transition, I come before You with a heart that sometimes feels uncertain and weary. I know that You see the end from the beginning, and I trust that You have a perfect plan for my life. Help me to find direction in Your Word. Motivate me in Your strength and give me courage through Your promises. Guide my steps and lead me as I navigate this new chapter. When I become weary, remind me that I am never alone and that You are for me and with me wherever I go. Fill me with Your peace, and let my heart be anchored in the hope of Your unchanging love.*

*In Jesus' name, I pray. Amen.*

# NAVIGATING SEASONS OF GROWTH AND CHANGE

Navigating change can be challenging because transitions often stretch us, but this is where the growth potential lies. While exhilarating, life's twists and turns can also be daunting. Yet, in these moments, we can find hope and optimism, knowing that each transition carries the potential for growth.

I've been there, my friend, many times, and I'm sure you have too. You know that feeling when you're caught between chapters? When you've already turned the page, but the next story hasn't started yet? It's strange being in this in-between place. Some days it feels like standing in the middle of a bridge too far from the familiar shore to turn back but not quite able to see the other side clearly. The old comfort zone is in the rearview mirror, but the new one is still under construction. We are in the middle of the story with chapters still being written.

These seasons of change, they're full of potential, right? I love how God works like that. Even when we're standing in the middle of chaos, wondering which way is up, He's got this divine GPS running, guiding us. His presence in these seasons reassures us that we're not alone and that there's a purpose in every transition.

Let's walk through this together. I want to share what I've discovered about leaning into these transitions with unwavering faith (even when your knees shake!) We'll talk about reading the signs He's placing in our path, tuning in to His whispers for our lives, and taking those brave steps forward—even when we can't see the entire staircase. Because here's the beautiful truth: these moments refine us, preparing us to be santificed and shaped into exactly who He designed us to be.

## Scriptural Foundation

*"For everything there is a season, and a time for every matter under heaven…"*

~ Ecclesiastes 3:1-8

*"From Issachar, men who understood the times and knew what Israel should do – 200 chiefs, with all their relatives under their command;"*

~ 1 Chronicles 12:32

*"Every good gift and every perfect gift is from above, coming down from the Father of lights, with whom there is no variation or shadow due to change."*

~ James 1:17

*"Behold, I am doing a new thing; now it springs forth, do you not perceive it? I will make a way in the wilderness and rivers in the desert."*

~ Isaiah 43:19

## Navigating Seasons and Transitions

Our lives are marked by a series of transitions, dreams, and seasons, each holding the potential for growth, change, and the pursuit of new endeavors. God has uniquely designed each season of life with specific callings and purposes for us. From our earliest days, as we take our first steps and discover the world, the seeds of dreams are planted in our hearts. These dreams, in our youth, are limitless. As children, we are free to dream without the constraints of reality or self-doubt. We imagine ourselves as astronauts, explorers, doctors, and artists, embracing those possibilities with wide-eyed wonder.

> *Our lives are marked by a series of transitions, dreams, and seasons, each holding the potential for growth, change, and the pursuit of new endeavors.*

I recently talked with my great-niece about what she wants to be when she grows up. Without hesitation and with the purest of enthusiasm, she said, "I want to be an actress and a veterinarian or maybe both!" In her young mind, the possibilities are endless, and the sky is the limit. We encourage kids to pursue their dreams and believe in their potential. I wish we could always live with child-like faith in a world that doesn't impose limitations on us.

However, as we journey through life, we inevitably encounter opposition. The road to fulfilling our calling and growing in faith is often fraught with challenges. It requires perseverance, hard work, grit, and an unwavering commitment to the path God has set before us. Perseverance isn't just about getting through tough times and growing through them. It's a testament to our determination and resilience. Each struggle we face is an opportunity to deepen our faith and reliance on God. When we persevere, we build character, and that character produces hope—a hope that doesn't disappoint because it's rooted in God's unfailing love.

> *Each struggle we face is an opportunity to deepen our faith and reliance on God.*

Oftentimes, we begin our journey with the best intentions, filled with excitement and purpose, but then we hit the "messy middle." This is the season when doubts creep in, and we find ourselves questioning whether we can continue, or we may even contemplate giving up altogether. The messy middle is a difficult place of transition. It's where the initial excitement wears off, and the reality of the hard work ahead sets in. It's where we must face our fears, doubts, and insecurities.

We start to question our abilities, self-worth, and even the legitimacy of our dreams. It's easy to play it safe, retreat to the familiar, and convince ourselves that staying put is better than risking failure. We hear the inner critic telling us we're not good enough or that our dreams are too big. Sometimes, even well-meaning friends and family may unintentionally discourage us from pursuing our calling, not out of malice but from their own fears and concerns for us.

But what if we decided to ignore the naysayers? What if we dared to step out in faith and listen solely to the voice of our Heavenly Father? What if we started to pray big, bold, and audacious prayers for our lives, believing that God has planted those dreams in our hearts for a reason?

## Understanding the Seasons

The book of Ecclesiastes tells us there is a season for everything. Ecclesiastes 3:1-8 says,

> *For everything there is a season, and a time for every matter under heaven:*
> *a time to be born and a time to die;*
> *a time to plant, and a time to pluck up what is planted;*
> *a time to kill, and a time to heal;*
> *a time to break down, and a time to build up;*
> *a time to weep, and a time to laugh;*
> *a time to mourn, and a time to dance;*
> *a time to cast away stones, and a time to gather stones together;*
> *a time to embrace, and a time to refrain from embracing;*
> *a time to seek, and a time to lose;*
> *a time to keep, and a time to cast away;*
> *a time to tear, and a time to sew;*
> *a time to keep silence, and a time to speak;*
> *a time to love, and a time to hate;*
> *a time for war, and a time for peace.*

Seasons are an integral part of life for farmers; they determine when crops can be planted and harvested. Understanding the importance of seasons helps gardeners and farmers maximize their yield.

> *Understanding our seasons allows us to create a harvest in our lives, too!*

Understanding our seasons allows us to create a harvest in our lives, too! When seasons change, they are a beautiful reminder of God's constant presence in our lives, marking a time for preparation and celebration.

As we navigate seasons of growth and change, we have an incredible opportunity to embrace the transformation with joy and excitement that comes with each new chapter. Whether we're stepping into a season of abundant harvest or facing a time of pruning, we can trust that God is at work, refining us and preparing us for what lies ahead.

We experience many different seasons throughout our lifetimes. Just as the earth renews itself with each passing season, we, too, are given the opportunity to grow, adapt, and align ourselves more closely with God's purpose for our lives. We should view this shift as a time to celebrate His faithfulness and prepare our hearts for the new opportunities He sets before us.

## Navigating Seasons and Transitions

The Jewish faith is rich in tradition, especially in its celebration of religious festivals that beautifully intertwine with the changing seasons. As I've studied these sacred rhythms, I've discovered how deeply they resonate with my Christian walk.

Each season on the Jewish calendar brings unique ceremonies and celebrations, all tied to the earth's natural cycles. From the vibrant renewal of Passover in the spring to the reflective beginning of Rosh Hashanah in the autumn, the seasons play a crucial role in these observances. The Jewish calendar, rooted in a lunar cycle, aligns many holy days with the rhythms of the natural world. For instance, Passover heralds spring's arrival, a time when the earth awakens and new life blossoms. Similarly, Rosh Hashanah coincides with the onset of autumn, a season marked by falling leaves and shorter days. However, it also signals the start of a new year and a time for renewal and reflection.

These seasonal transitions are significant not just in religious practices but also in agricultural ones. Farmers must be attuned to the timing and rhythm of the seasons. They carefully plan when to plant and harvest, understanding that the success of their crops depends on factors such as soil, water, temperature, and sunlight. In the same way, we must intentionally plant good seeds in our leadership and nurture habits that will yield the kind of fruit we desire in our lives. With intentionality, we, too, can look forward to reaping a bountiful harvest in the coming seasons.

Just as the seasons bring both change and new opportunities, so do the transitions in our lives and leadership. Embrace them with faith, knowing that each has its purpose, and that with God's guidance, we can navigate them with wisdom and grace.

## Embracing the Messy Middle: Where Real Growth Takes Root

The hardest part is realizing that transformation doesn't follow a neat timeline. Seeds take time to grow. There are days when you feel like you're making giant leaps forward, and others when you're left wondering if you're moving at all. On my leadership journey, I'm learning that growth occurs in the questions, in the quiet moments of doubt, and in the small victories that go unnoticed by others. It's in the late-night conversations with yourself, the mistakes that teach

*The hardest part is realizing that transformation doesn't follow a neat timeline.*

you more than successes ever could, and the gradual realization that discomfort is where the magic happens.

And you know what? It's okay to sit with this uncertainty. To acknowledge that growth isn't always Instagram-worthy. Sometimes, it's just you showing up each day and doing your best to figure things out one small decision at a time. There's no highlight reel for the moments when you're reimagining yourself, no filter for the raw authenticity of 'becoming.'

## Understand the Times

Friends, we must understand the times and seasons. We live in a critical hour on the Kingdom Calendar, and God has specific work for us to do today at this hour. We, like the sons of Issachar, need to understand the times and seasons we were living in. *"...from Issachar, men who understood the times and knew what Israel should do – 200 chiefs, with all their relatives under their command...."* 1 Chronicles 12:32

*We live in a critical hour on the Kingdom Calendar, and God has specific work for us to do today at this hour.*

Time is short. We need everyone in the kingdom of God suited up to take their place in the kingdom to proclaim the good news of Jesus, His death, burial, and resurrection. We are in the last days. We've lived in the last days since Pentecost and know Jesus is returning soon. We don't know the day or hour, but we can see the signs and seasons.

We've been chosen to live in the end days, before the second coming of Jesus Christ. His return is imminent. Therefore, we must be watchful and wait as we prepare for His return. Living in the last days means living with a sense of urgency as we prioritize the salvation of the lost and our spiritual growth, while loving and serving others.

What a privilege we have been given to share the gospel message as a witness for Christ, grounded in both truth and love. We must remain alert and be aware of the signs of the end times as described in the Bible. We need to be ready to stand firm and face the world with faith and confidence in God's plan and our purpose.

## Managing our Schedules

One way to be intentional in every season is to recognize that being a good steward doesn't always involve adding items to our schedule. Sometimes, pursuing our calling requires pruning and eliminating things—even good, God-honoring activities! As we navigate changing seasons in our pursuit of our God-given purpose, it's essential for our gifts and calling to align with our current season.

God often plants a dream in our hearts long before it comes to fruition. That's why it's crucial to understand our season and what God asks us to do during each one. We may have a calling to lead, write, speak, podcast, start a business, or pursue any number of things, but it might not be our season. This is why reflecting on your calling during every season is essential.

> *God often plants a dream in our hearts long before it comes to fruition.*

It's crucial to recognize that every season of life brings both challenges and opportunities. In our journey as leaders, seasons of growth and change can often feel overwhelming. Living intentionally helps us discern what God wants us to focus on during each phase of life. It's about being present in the moment, aligning our actions with God's purposes, and not rushing ahead or lagging behind His timing. I've been guilty of getting ahead in excitement, but I would much rather attune myself to the Holy Spirit's guidance and rhythm. Whether it's a time for growth, rest, or transition, living intentionally in each season ensures we make the most of every moment. Most importantly, it means fully embracing God's plan for our lives in every season, surrendering to His will, and trusting in His perfect timing.

One of the key ways to navigate these transitions is by intentionally managing our schedules. Just as a gardener prunes a tree to remove dead branches and allow for new growth, we, too, must periodically evaluate our commitments and responsibilities. Pruning may involve letting go of activities or even relationships that no longer serve our purpose or align with the direction God is leading us. By doing so, we create space for new opportunities and growth. Managing our time wisely and pruning our schedules can help us stay focused on what truly matters, ensuring that we invest our energy where it will yield the most fruit. In these seasons, remember that God often uses change to bring about new life and greater abundance in our leadership and personal lives.

## Personal Practices on Time Management

I manage my schedule and time by being intentional and prayerful about my commitments. On my best day, I begin with quiet time, seeking God's guidance for the day ahead. Setting priorities aligned with my purpose and calling is essential to living my best life. I use a combination of time-blocking and task prioritization to ensure that my most important work gets done while still leaving room for flexibility and rest.

During my tenure with Spark Media, I streamlined my content creation process by shifting from scheduling and recording weekly podcast interviews to batch recording my content a few times a year. During these dedicated periods, I focus intensely on recording, sometimes producing as many as 20 podcast episodes over just a few days. This approach allowed me to maximize my productivity and maintain a consistent content schedule without the weekly time pressure. By batching my content creation, I freed up more time throughout the year to focus on other aspects of my work and ministry while ensuring that my podcast remains fresh and engaging.

I also learned the power of saying no to activities that don't align with my goals and purposes. By pruning unnecessary commitments, I can focus more effectively on what truly matters. This disciplined approach helps me balance my roles and responsibilities while being centered on my faith and mission. So what is God wanting from you in this season, my friend?

# APPLICATION QUESTIONS

How have you seen your calling and gifts align with different seasons of your life?

..................................................................................................

..................................................................................................

..................................................................................................

..................................................................................................

..................................................................................................

Can you share an experience where a shift in season led to a new understanding or pursuit of your calling?

..................................................................................................

..................................................................................................

..................................................................................................

..................................................................................................

..................................................................................................

The chapter mentions the "messy middle," where doubts and opposition arise. How have you navigated through this phase in your life? What strategies or support systems helped you overcome these challenges?

................................................................................

................................................................................

................................................................................

................................................................................

................................................................................

What bold prayers have you prayed in the past, and how did they shape your journey? How can you incorporate this practice more consistently into your current season?

................................................................................

................................................................................

................................................................................

................................................................................

................................................................................

How do you discern God's timing for different assignments or projects in your life?

..................................................................................................
..................................................................................................
..................................................................................................
..................................................................................................
..................................................................................................
..................................................................................................

What signs or confirmations do you seek to understand if pursuing a particular dream or goal is the right season?

..................................................................................................
..................................................................................................
..................................................................................................
..................................................................................................
..................................................................................................
..................................................................................................

Ecclesiastes 3:1-8 speaks to the different times and seasons in life. How do these verses resonate with your current season? How can you align your faith and actions to make the most of this season according to God's plan?

.................................................................................................

.................................................................................................

.................................................................................................

.................................................................................................

.................................................................................................

# PRAYER

*Heavenly Father,*

*Thank You for the seasons You bring into our lives, each with its unique purpose and lessons. Help us to understand and embrace the season we are in, trusting that Your timing is perfect. Grant us the wisdom to align our gifts and callings with Your plans. Strengthen us to face opposition with faith and perseverance, and guide us to bold and audacious prayers. May we always seek Your voice above all others and step forward with courage and confidence in Your divine purpose for us.*

*In Jesus' name, we pray. Amen.*

# Finishing Strong And Leaving A Legacy

As Christian women in leadership, we want to finish our race strong. We long to hear the words, "Well done, my good and faithful servant." So, we live with intention, exercising our faith and casting a vision far beyond our lives. Legacy is not about the fleeting accolades or temporary successes we achieve; it is about what endures, the seeds we plant that will grow into trees we may never sit under. It's about the inheritance of faith, wisdom, and love that we pass down to the next generation, shaping their lives and pointing them toward God's purpose.

The Word of God, our ultimate guide, reminds us in Deuteronomy 6:6-7 to diligently teach His commands to our children, letting His truths flow naturally in our daily lives and conversations. Discipleship, as outlined in Scripture, is the heart of legacy—living and leading in a way that leaves a lasting imprint on the lives of others.

Let's explore what it means to finish strong and leave a legacy rooted in Christ. Whether in our homes, workplaces, or communities, we can cultivate memories and build something that outlives us. Let's examine Scripture's timeless principles to help us build a legacy that glorifies God and enriches future generations.

## Scriptural Foundation

*"A good man leaves an inheritance to his children's children, but the sinner's wealth is laid up for the righteous."*

~ Proverbs 13:22

*"We will not hide them from their children, but tell to the coming generation the glorious deeds of the Lord, and his might, and the wonders that he has done."*

~ Psalm 78:4

*"And these words that I command you today shall be on your heart. You shall teach them diligently to your children, and shall talk of them when you sit in your house, and when you walk by the way, and when you lie down, and when you rise."*

~ Deuteronomy 6:6-7

### Leaving a Legacy

> **Legacy is our enduring mark, our influence reverberating through lives and generations even after we're gone.**

Legacy is not just about planting seeds in a garden you may never see harvested. It's about building something that will outlive you and extend far beyond your lifetime. Legacy is our enduring mark, our influence reverberating through lives and generations even after we're gone.

Let's dive deeper into the concept of legacy, what it truly is, why it matters, and how we can intentionally create one. We'll also explore specific ways to support our leadership, business, and ministry endeavors to leave a meaningful and enduring legacy.

## What Is a Legacy?

We all have some familiarity with the idea of a legacy, but how often do we pause to consider the legacy we are currently building? A legacy is something of value passed down from generation to generation, a gift or inheritance that carries significance and purpose. It is crafted through countless purposeful actions, often over years or even decades—loving those around you by investing your time, talents, and resources, living with integrity to be a trustworthy example, and wisely stewarding and growing what you've been given.

## Why Leave a Legacy?

Our influence will continue to shape and guide future generations when we leave a legacy. It's about creating a ripple effect that helps others embody the valuable life lessons you've learned. By leaving a legacy, you contribute to the future in a way that impacts lives you'll never meet, helping to pave the way for generations to come.

> *Our influence will continue to shape and guide future generations when we leave a legacy. It's*

My father-in-law left an incredible legacy, both personally and professionally. A tireless worker, he was a man of unwavering faith and integrity who loved his family deeply. With a dry sense of humor, he often shared cherished stories and imparted wisdom around the dinner table, creating moments we'll always treasure.

Under his leadership at a struggling Houston oil company, he confronted unethical environmental practices and refused to let them continue, guided by his deep moral convictions. He went on to transform Hilcorp Energy into an industry leader renowned for both integrity and excellence. The company's success and values were perhaps best exemplified when it awarded every employee a $100,000 bonus, a remarkable gesture that made headlines and demonstrated its commitment to sharing prosperity with its workforce.

My father-in-law, Pete Phillip, served Hilcorp faithfully until he passed away from brain cancer. In his eulogy, Jeff Hildebrand, the founder of Hilcorp, credited Pete with the company's success, highlighting his servant leadership and unwavering principles. This story exemplifies how a life lived with integrity and purpose can leave a legacy that inspires and blesses others long after we're gone.

Building a legacy involves the seeds we plant that will flourish in the lives of others. Through our actions, professional influence, and spiritual investments, we can create something that endures and makes a difference. A legacy is not just about wealth or status; it's the imprint of our lives on the hearts of others, the stories shared long after we're gone, and the values that will continue to guide future generations.

As women in leadership, we hold a distinctive position that allows us to shape a legacy reflecting our faith, love, and commitment to God's purpose. Let's delve into how we can finish strong and leave a lasting legacy in three key areas: personal, professional, and beyond ourselves.

## Our Personal Legacy: The Stories We Leave Behind

Our legacy is shaped by the choices we make, the stories we tell, and the wisdom we impart. It's the sum of our daily actions, relationships, and how we live out our faith in the most intimate circles of our lives: our families, friends, and communities. Each decision, whether big or small, contributes to the legacy we are building.

Who you are today is the result of the choices you've made and the actions you've taken. Each decision, each step forward, has shaped the person you've become. But it doesn't stop there. Who you aspire to be is equally important. Your vision for the future, the goals you set, and the values you hold dear all guide your journey forward.

> *Who you are today is the result of the choices you've made and the actions you've taken.*

Every moment and action contributes to the impact you leave behind, affecting not only your life but also the lives of those who come after you. The legacy you create mirrors the person you are and the person you aim to become.

## The Importance of Family Stories and Passing Down Wisdom

Think for a moment about the stories passed down in your own family. Perhaps it's the story of a grandparent who faced incredible hardship with unwavering faith or a parent who sacrificed much to ensure a better future for their children. These stories carry the essence of who they were and what they stood for. They continue to inspire and guide us long after they've gone.

As leaders, it's crucial that we are deliberate about the stories we pass down to the next generation. Are we sharing our experiences—both the triumphs and the trials—in ways that teach and inspire? Are we imparting the wisdom that God has given us through the various seasons of our lives? It's not just about the good times; it's about being transparent about our struggles, failures, and how God has worked in and through them.

Let's also consider the importance of family history. Our children and grandchildren need to know where they come from, not just biologically but spiritually and culturally. Sharing family history is more than just recounting events; it's about passing down values, faith, and a sense of identity rooted in God's purpose.

> *The wisdom we impart is one of the greatest gifts we can leave behind.*

Finally, the wisdom we impart is one of the greatest gifts we can leave behind. Proverbs 13:22 reminds us that *"a good man leaves an inheritance to his children's children."* This inheritance is not just material wealth but includes the wisdom and spiritual wealth needed to guide them through their lives. Let us be diligent in teaching the next generation the ways of the Lord, equipping them with the tools they need to navigate life's challenges with faith and integrity.

## Professional Legacy: Influence and Inspiration in the Workplace

Our professional legacy is not measured by our job title, financial success, or the accolades we receive. While these may be markers of achievement, they are not an accurate measure of our legacy.

Instead, our professional legacy lies in our influence on others and the inspiration we provide to those who walk alongside us in the workplace. It is less about our words and more about how we make inspire them and make them feel.

As women of faith, we are called to live out our beliefs in every area of our lives, including our careers. This means treating others with kindness, fairness, and respect, regardless of their position or status. It means leading with integrity, making decisions that honor God, and standing firm in our values even when it is difficult. Our professional legacy is shaped by how we conduct ourselves daily, build relationships, and uplift others.

Consider the people you work with or have worked with in the past. How have you influenced them? Have you been a source of encouragement, a mentor, or a role model? Have you used your position to empower others, especially those just starting their careers? Bringing others along on your journey is one of the most impactful ways to build a lasting professional legacy. It's not just about your success; it is about how you've helped others succeed and grow in their own right.

Moreover, your professional legacy reflects how you have integrated your faith into your work. Colossians 3:23 reminds us, *"Whatever you do, work heartily, as for the Lord and not for men."* When we approach our work with this mindset, our professional legacy becomes a testimony of our faith, showing others that it is possible to succeed in business while staying true to God's principles.

## Legacy Beyond Ourselves: Planting Seeds for Future Generations

Legacy is not just about what we leave behind; it's about our impact on future generations, even those we may never meet. The saying,

*Legacy is not just about what we leave behind; it's about our impact on future generations,*

"Wise men plant trees they'll never sit under" speaks to the selfless act of building a legacy that benefits vothers long after we're gone. As leaders, we must think beyond our lifetime and consider how we are setting up a fruitful and honorable legacy for our children, their children, and beyond.

This legacy goes beyond personal and professional achievements; it's about the faith and charitable works we instill in future generations. What kind of example are we setting in our relationship with God? Are we showing the next generation what it means to live a life of faith, service, and love? Are we investing in their spiritual growth, teaching them to seek God's will in all things, and encouraging them to serve others with compassion and humility?

One of the most profound ways to leave a legacy beyond ourselves is through acts of charity and service. When we invest in causes that align with God's heart—whether by caring for the poor, supporting missions, or advocating for justice—we plant seeds that will bear fruit long after we're gone. These acts of kindness and service create a ripple effect, touching lives we may never know and inspiring others to continue the work we've begun.

Let us also consider the importance of prayer in building a legacy. Our prayers have the power to influence generations, shaping the lives of our descendants in ways we cannot even imagine. As women of faith, we must commit to praying for our children, grandchildren, and those who will come after them, asking God to guide, protect, and bless them as they carry forward the legacy we have begun.

Finishing strong and leaving a legacy requires intentionality, faith, and a commitment to living out God's purpose in every area of our lives. Whether through the stories we share, our influence in our professional lives, or the seeds we plant for future generations, our legacy reflects our walk with God and our impact on others. Let's be intentional in our living, knowing that the legacy we leave will profoundly shape the future. May we all strive to finish strong, leaving a legacy that honors God and blesses those who follow in our footsteps.

As Christian women in leadership, we have unique opportunities to make a lasting impact in the lives of others, both in our personal circles and our professional spheres. Here are several specific ways you can leave a legacy that honors God and inspires future generations.

## Cultivating a Culture of Generosity

Generosity is a hallmark of a life well-lived and a key component of a lasting legacy. My husband, Peter, exudes generosity. He has taught me much about giving to those in need and trusting God to provide for everything. As leaders, we can model and cultivate a culture of generosity within our organizations, churches, and communities. This could be through financial giving, but it also includes giving our time, talents, and resources to those in need. Whether it's supporting missions, funding scholarships, or volunteering for charitable causes, these acts of generosity leave a lasting imprint on the hearts and lives of those we help.

## Living Out Your Faith Boldly

Our testimonies are powerful tools for leaving a legacy. Rooted in Revelation 12:11, where it states, *"... and they have conquered him by the blood of the Lamb and by the word of their testimony...."* we see that our stories of faith, perseverance, and God's work in our lives hold the power to inspire, encourage, and uplift others. Sharing how we have overcome challenges and witnessed God's grace glorifies Him and becomes a lasting imprint on the hearts of those we impact. This legacy, anchored in the truth of what God has done, can influence future generations, reminding them of our victory in Christ and encouraging them to walk boldly in their faith journeys.

Your testimony and how you live out your faith daily can profoundly impact those around you. Be unapologetically bold in your faith, whether in the workplace, community, or home. This could mean starting a prayer group at work, sharing your faith story in a public setting, or simply being known as someone who stands firm in her beliefs. When others see your courage and conviction, they are inspired to live their faith with the same boldness.

> *Your testimony and how you live out your faith daily can profoundly impact those around you.*

## Writing, Speaking, & Podcasting to Inspire Others

Writing, speaking, and podcasting are powerful avenues through which we can inspire others and leave a lasting legacy. Each word shared through these mediums has the potential to touch hearts, spark change, and encourage others in their own journeys. Whether through a written page, a spoken message, or a podcast episode, these platforms allow us to share our stories, insights, and wisdom with a broader audience.

If God has given you the gift of communication, consider using it to write or speak about your experiences, lessons learned, and the ways God has moved in your life. Writing a book, starting a blog or podcast, or speaking at conferences can extend your influence beyond your immediate circle. Your words can touch the lives of countless people, offering them encouragement, wisdom, and insight they can carry with them throughout their journey.

By boldly expressing our faith, experiences, and lessons learned, we influence those who hear or read our words, creating a ripple effect extending beyond our lifetime. This legacy of inspiration can empower others to live out their calling, embrace their God-given purpose, and continue the cycle of encouragement for generations to come.

## Creating a Legacy of Prayer

Never underestimate the power of prayer in building a legacy. By consistently praying for your family, community, and colleagues, you are sowing seeds that will bear fruit for generations. You can also leave a legacy of prayer by teaching others how to pray, leading prayer groups, or even writing down your prayers for your children and grandchildren to cherish and learn. Prayer is a powerful tool that connects us to God's will and purpose. It is one of the most impactful ways we can leave a lasting mark.

> *Never underestimate the power of prayer in building a legacy.*

Finally, consider how you can invest in kingdom work that will outlive you. This might involve supporting Christian education, church planting efforts, or funding ministries to share the gospel globally. By aligning your resources with God's work, you ensure that your legacy is not just temporal but eternal, making a difference for generations in ways that only God can fully measure.

# APPLICATION QUESTIONS

Reflect on the stories and wisdom passed down to you. How have they shaped your life and faith?

..................................................................................................................

..................................................................................................................

..................................................................................................................

..................................................................................................................

..................................................................................................................

In your professional life, how are you influencing and inspiring others? What legacy do you hope to leave in your field?

..................................................................................................................

..................................................................................................................

..................................................................................................................

..................................................................................................................

..................................................................................................................

How are you investing in future generations within your family and beyond? What seeds are you planting today that will bear fruit in the future?

.................................................................................................

.................................................................................................

.................................................................................................

.................................................................................................

.................................................................................................

What role does prayer play in the legacy you are building? How can you incorporate more intentional prayer for future generations into your life?

.................................................................................................

.................................................................................................

.................................................................................................

.................................................................................................

.................................................................................................

# PRAYER

*Heavenly Father,*

*Thank You for the opportunity to build a legacy that reflects Your love, grace, and truth. Please help us live each day intentionally, knowing that our actions, words, and decisions can shape the future. Guide us as we pass down wisdom and stories to the next generation, and empower us to influence and inspire others professionally. May our legacy honor You and bless those who come after us.*

*In Jesus' name, we pray. Amen.*

# Notes

# Answering The Call

As we come to these final moments on our journey together to spark influence and lead with boldness, purpose, and passion, I commission you to go in faith boldly. I also want to remind you that you are here for a reason. You are not a mistake; your life is no accident. God has placed specific gifts, talents, and passions within you—not just for your fulfillment but for advancing His Kingdom. Your calling could be in leadership, teaching, serving, or any other area where you can use your unique gifts to glorify God.

Friend, the time has come to take everything we've explored and learned throughout these pages and let it ignite your soul to live with passion and purpose. You are commissioned to shine brightly, set apart, consecrated for extraordinary works, not to blend in, but to step boldly into the calling God has prepared for you.

Walking in your God-given calling isn't just checking off tasks or chasing worldly accomplishments. It's about something far greater and more profound. When we surrender our hearts to Him and do His will, we can glorify God through every action, every

> *Walking in your God-given calling isn't just checking off tasks or chasing worldly accomplishments*

choice, and every moment of our lives. It's about allowing His light to radiate through us, bringing hope, joy, and transformation to those around us. Living with purpose means recognizing that every step of the journey—every victory, every challenge, and every lesson—has been preparing you for this exact season.

*Boldness means trusting God when the path ahead seems unclear.*

But let me be clear. This journey requires boldness. Not the kind of boldness that relies on your own strength or abilities but a boldness fueled by faith, a faith that rests securely in the One who calls you. Boldness means trusting God when the path ahead seems unclear. It means stepping forward even when fear whispers to you to hold back. It means declaring with confidence, "Here I am, Lord. Send me."

Together, we'll unpack what it means to spark your passion and live with intentional purpose. This final chapter invites you to embrace who God has created you to be and lead with courage, authenticity, and unwavering trust in His call on your life and His great plan. The world desperately needs believers who will not fear but who will rise up, step out, and live boldly for the glory of God. You have a light to share, a message to proclaim, and a purpose to fulfill. Let's take this next step together, walking boldly in faith and inspiring others to do the same.

## Scriptural Foundation

*"'You are the light of the world. A city set on a hill cannot be hidden. Nor do people light a lamp and put it under a basket, but on a stand, and it gives light to all in the house. In the same way, let your light shine before others, so that they may see your good works and give glory to your Father who is in heaven."*

~ Matthew 5:14-16

*"If we live by the Spirit, let us also keep in step with the Spirit."*

~ Galatians 5:25

*"And let us consider how to stir up one another to love and good works."*

~ Hebrews 10:24

## Spark Your Passion & Live with Purpose

As we conclude this transformative journey together, it's time to apply all we've learned to boldly walk in our God-given calling. Throughout this book, I've shared how the Lord has uniquely crafted us with specific gifts, talents, and passions to use in His Kingdom. Walking in your calling isn't just about fulfilling tasks or achieving goals. It's about living with passion and purpose every single day for the glory of God. By fully embracing our calling and living in the fullness of who

God created us to be, we become a living testament to God's grace, creativity, power, and love, inspiring others to do the same.

God didn't create you randomly; He designed you with a unique purpose. Your life and purpose are an incredible journey of discovery, with all its experiences, challenges, and victories. Everything has been preparing you for this very moment. God has already inscribed your purpose on your heart, but it is up to you to discover it and boldly go where He calls you.

*Boldness doesn't mean fearlessness*

Boldness doesn't mean fearlessness. It means moving forward despite fear and trusting that God is with you every step of the way. It's time to stand up with courage and conviction, stepping into every area God calls you to lead. The enemy will try to sow seeds of doubt, but you can stand firm, knowing that God's power is greater than any obstacle you face. Boldness doesn't mean we won't experience fear; rather, it's about being rooted in God's love. With a heart filled with humility and love, we can boldly go where God leads, empowering others to do the same.

Fully living with purpose and passion requires a proactive stance. It is what Eugene Peterson calls a long obedience in the same direction. This lifestyle of bold faith is about taking deliberate steps toward what God has placed in your heart, even when it doesn't make sense to others. This means listening to God's voice and acting on it, pushing past the doubts and fears that threaten to hold you back. It's about being determined and committed to living in bold faith, inspiring others to do the same.

The word 'go' in all its forms in the Bible is used more than 1500 times. We are to go into all the world sharing the Gospel and radiating His love. When we declare, "Here I am, Lord, send me," we can move forward with the confidence that He will provide everything we need. He will give us the wisdom, the resources, the provision, strength, and everything we need for the journey.

The beautiful thing about living in the fullness of who He created us to be is that it becomes contagious when we choose to live with bold faith. When we step out in faith, it transforms our lives and inspires others to do the same. This is how we spark influence. Our boldness ignites sparks in others to do what God has called them to do. Walking in our assignments encourages others to follow their callings with courage and faith. When we walk boldly in our callings, we become a beacon of hope and a living testimony of God's power and faithfulness to others, proving that all things are possible with Him.

> *Our boldness ignites sparks in others to do what God has called them to do.*

## Stepping Out in Faith

Stepping out in faith, especially in leadership, often requires courage and trust in a plan that isn't always visible. I've experienced this firsthand many times in my life, whether in homeschooling my kids, launching a podcast, hosting events, changing careers, or writing books. God has shown me to trust His plan even when unsure of how it will work out. I've repeatedly seen how trusting in God's direction and taking bold, sometimes uncertain steps can lead to a life rich with adventure and purpose. I hope you will have the same boldness, even when unprepared. Answering God's call isn't without its challenges. I urge you to push past the fear, anchor yourself to God's promises, and surround yourself with people who uplift and encourage you to be all God desires.

> *Leadership, especially when rooted in faith, demands intentional action.*

Leadership, especially when rooted in faith, demands intentional action. Success occurs when we break the journey into manageable steps and purposeful actions. Daily Bible reading and meditation are crucial for staying aligned with God's will. Throughout the book, I've proposed practical steps, such as setting aside time for prayer and reflection to seek God's guidance, creating a vision board to clarify goals, and forming accountability partnerships with like-minded believers to cheer us on.

My leadership journey has been shaped by the wisdom of mentors and the strength of faith-filled friends who support and encourage me. I urge you to seek out mentors and build a supportive community to help you grow in your calling. My goal is always to lead by example, whether in business, on social media, through my podcasts, books, or speaking engagements; I strive to live out my calling with boldness and authenticity. By sharing my journey transparently, I hope to inspire you to step out in faith, make bold moves, and lead with courage.

## Now It's Your Turn to Spark Others

Your calling isn't just about you; it's about how God wants to use you to impact the lives of others. Your boldness catalyzes those around you to step into their God-given purposes. As you passionately embrace your calling, you will naturally inspire others to do the same. Let me tell you the joy of seeing others embrace their God-given purposes and assignments because of your obedience is a source of immense fulfillment.

*Your calling isn't just about you; it's about how God wants to use you to impact the lives of others.*

## Salt and Light

In these times, more than ever, we are called to rise and live boldly as salt and light in a world that desperately needs the hope and truth of Christ and His love. The cultural landscape is shifting rapidly, with values that were once foundational now being questioned or even discarded. As followers of Jesus, we are not called to blend in but to stand out—to be the seasoning that preserves God's truth and the light that shines brightly in the darkness. Jesus commissioned us to be the salt of the earth and the light of the world, urging us to let our light shine before others so they may see our good works and give glory to our Father in heaven.

Matthew 5:14-16 says, *"You are the light of the world. A city set on a hill cannot be hidden. Nor do people light a lamp and put it under a basket, but on a stand, and it gives light to all in the house. In the same way, let your light shine before others, so that they may see your good works and give glory to your Father who is in heaven."* This verse reminds us of our role as believers to shine brightly and not hide our God-given gifts and calling. When you boldly walk in your calling, you become a beacon of hope, guiding others to their God-given destinies.

Living boldly as salt and light isn't just an option for us as believers; it's a necessity in these days. Our world is crying out for truth, for hope, and for the transformative power of God's love. Every day, we encounter people who are searching for meaning, grappling with brokenness, and longing for something greater than what this world offers. As salt, we are called to preserve what is good and true, to stand firm in our convictions, and to flavor the culture around us with the love and wisdom of Christ. As light, we are called to push back the darkness, bring clarity where there is confusion, and guide others toward the life-giving truth of the Gospel. I love the way Pastor Allen Jackson shared this with me in an interview. "We are to be salt and light, not light salt."

## Courageous Faith Through Speaking Truth with Love and Conviction

We can no longer afford to be passive or complacent in our faith. The forces of darkness are active, seeking to erode the moral fabric of our society, silence the voice of truth, and destroy all that is good. If we shrink back in fear or fade into the background, we risk losing our influence and failing to fulfill the mission that Christ has entrusted to us.

*Now is the time to rise with courage, speak the truth in love, and live out our faith with conviction and integrity.*

Now is the time to rise with courage, speak the truth in love, and live out our faith with conviction and integrity. The impact we can have as salt and light is profound; it will transform hearts, shift cultural norms, and point others to the eternal hope found in Jesus.

It is essential for the next generation to see us walking in the fullness of God's will. Young people today are growing up in a world where truth is often seen as relative, and moral absolutes are under constant attack. They need to see authentic examples of faith and love lived out with passion and purpose. They need to witness believers who are unafraid to stand for what is right, willing to engage with the culture in meaningful ways, and committed to making a difference for the Kingdom of God. Our boldness in living out our faith will inspire them to do the same, equipping them to be salt and light in their own spheres of influence.

Let's remember that the days we live in demand a bold and unashamed witness for Christ. As the world grows darker, the light of Christ within us must shine even brighter. We are called to be difference makers to influence the culture, impact lives, and be the hands and feet of Jesus in a world that desperately needs His love.

So, friends, let's not shrink back but step forward with confidence, knowing that God has equipped us to be salt and light, to preserve what is good, to dispel the darkness, and to point others to the hope we have in Him. Now is the time to live boldly for Christ, making an eternal impact on the world around us.

## Inspire Others Along the Way

Don't keep your story to yourself. Inspire others by sharing your journey. When you authentically share your story with others—both the struggles and the victories—your transparency will encourage others who may be walking a similar path.

*Inspire others by sharing your journey.*

Look for opportunities to mentor others, especially younger women who are just beginning to discover the call on their life. Offer your wisdom, encouragement, and support as they navigate their own journeys. Then rejoice in the successes of others. When you see someone else walking boldly in their calling, celebrate them! Your genuine support will create a culture of encouragement and mutual growth.

## Embrace a Lifelong Journey to Walk in Step with the Spirit

Remember, friend, walking in your calling is not a one-time decision but a lifelong journey. Your calling may evolve as you grow, and God may lead you to new and unexpected places. The key is to stay in step with the Spirit and allow Him to guide your every move.

Galatians 5:25 encourages us, *"If we live by the Spirit, let us also keep in step with the Spirit."* This means continually seeking God's guidance, being open to His leading, and trusting Him with every aspect of your journey.

Your purpose and calling is a journey, not a destination. Stay in step with the Spirit, and He will lead you to places you never imagined. To stay in step with the Spirit, cultivate a daily walk with God. Spend time each day in prayer, worship, and Bible study. This daily connection will keep you aligned with God's will. Then, remain teachable and always be willing to learn and grow. Be open to correction, new insights, and the leading of the Holy Spirit. Remember that God's

> *Your purpose and calling is a journey, not a destination.*

timing is perfect. Be patient and trust that He will fulfill His purposes in your life at the right time.

## Ideas to Spark Your Leadership Journey

Walking boldly in your calling often involves stepping into leadership roles, where you can use your God-given gifts to serve others and influence the culture around you. Here are some specific ways you can embrace leadership and create a significant impact on the world around you.

## Family Leadership

Leadership within the family is foundational and often overlooked. Whether you're raising children, supporting a spouse, or caring for aging parents, your role as a leader in the home is vital. Women, we are created to be our husband's helpmeet. Let's embrace this role with excellence in all we do. Family leadership involves modeling Christlike love, humility, and service to others daily. It's about creating a home environment where faith is nurtured, values are taught, and relationships are strengthened. Your leadership in the family can lay a spiritual foundation that will influence generations to come, making it one of the most significant leadership roles you can hold. Don't take this sphere of influence for granted; your home is your mission field.

## Mentorship and Calling Out Leadership

Mentorship is more than just sharing advice; it's about walking alongside someone as they navigate their journey. By becoming a mentor to younger women in your community or church, you're not only investing in their personal and spiritual growth but also helping them recognize and cultivate their own God-given gifts. I remember as a young mom asking a woman I respected to mentor me. I was shocked and disheartened when she told me no. Whether she was overwhelmed or intimidated, I'm not sure. I didn't need a grand program or serious hand holding; I simply needed a woman willing to meet with me for coffee and share her wisdom.

I have another friend who called leadership out in me, and this emboldened me to step out. Calling leadership out in others is a powerful act of encouragement and empowerment. Recognizing the God-given potential within someone and speaking life into that potential helps them to see the capabilities they may not fully recognize in themselves.

*Calling leadership out in others is a powerful act of encouragement and empowerment.*

Wendie Pett did just that for me, seeing the seeds of leadership in me and calling them forth at a Christian Women in Media Leadership Summit. By affirming my gifts and challenging me to step into greater roles of influence, Wendie not only encouraged my growth, but also set me on a path to impact countless others through my leadership. This act of calling out leadership has a ripple effect and is a testament to the profound influence we can have on others when we recognize, call out, and nurture their strengths.

## Lead Small Groups or Bible Studies

Use your passion for God's Word to lead a small group or Bible study. Leading a small group or Bible study offers a unique opportunity to nurture a community centered on God's Word. It's an opportunity to create a space where people feel safe to explore their faith, ask difficult questions, and support one another through life's challenges. As a leader, you have the opportunity to guide discussions to help others apply Scripture to their daily lives. This role provides an opportunity to model servant leadership. As you prioritize the needs and spiritual well-being of others, you help them grow in their relationship with God.

## Creative Leadership

Creative leadership is about using your gifts and talents to glorify God and inspire others. Whether you're a writer, musician, designer, artist, or business owner, you have the ability to communicate powerful messages through your work.

*Creative leadership is about using your gifts and talents to glorify God and inspire others.*

Leading workshops, creating spaces, platforms, and content, or collaborating with other creatives allows you to influence culture in a way that reflects God's beauty, truth, and goodness. Creative leadership is not just about showcasing your talents; it's about fostering environments where others can encounter God, explore their creativity, and find hope.

## Entrepreneurship

Entrepreneurship provides a platform to lead with integrity and purpose in the marketplace. By starting a business that reflects your Christian values, you have the chance to influence the business world with principles such as honesty, fairness, and compassion. As an entrepreneur, you can create jobs, develop innovative solutions to problems, and use your business as a force for good. Leadership in this area also entails mentoring other Christian entrepreneurs, sharing your journey, and assisting them in navigating the challenges of upholding faith-based values in a competitive marketplace.

## Public Speaking and Teaching

Public speaking and teaching are powerful ways to influence others and share the message of Christ. If you're gifted in communication, consider using this talent to speak at conferences, churches, or community events. Sharing your testimony, teaching biblical principles, and offering practical insights can inspire and equip others to live out their faith boldly. This type of leadership involves not just speaking to audiences but also connecting with them on a personal level, understanding their struggles, and offering hope and encouragement that resonates deeply.

## Advocacy and Community Involvement

Leadership in advocacy is about aligning your actions with God's heart for the enslaved and oppressed. Whether you're passionate about ending human trafficking, supporting the homeless, or caring for the least of these, your leadership can bring about genuine change. By leading a non-profit, organizing initiatives, rallying others to join the cause, and speaking out against injustices in a way that reflects Christ's love and compassion. When you lead in these areas, you become a voice for the voiceless, demonstrating how faith in action can transform society.

Community involvement is a practical way to lead by example and have a tangible impact in your local area. Whether you're volunteering, serving on a board, or organizing events, your leadership can bring people together, address local needs, and foster a sense of unity. By getting involved, you also have the opportunity to build relationships with others outside of your immediate circle, extending Christ's love and compassion to your broader community. Leading in this way not only helps others, but also strengthens your own faith as you see God working through you to create positive change.

Remember that you are uniquely created for a purpose. Embrace your calling with boldness and passion, trusting that God is with you every step of the way. Let His light shine through you as you walk confidently in the path He has set before you. The world needs the gifts only you can offer. Step out and let your light shine!

> *Remember that you are uniquely created for a purpose*

# Notes

# Final Thoughts

As I reflect on my journey from faith to action, I am reminded of the countless opportunities where God has guided my steps and provided the strength to pursue the calling He placed on my life in my mid-forties. It is never too late to begin. No matter our age or stage in life, God's calling never expires. We are never too old to take steps toward a new journey.

> *No matter our age or stage in life, God's calling never expires.*

Scripture is filled with examples of individuals who embarked on significant missions later in life. Abraham was called to be the father of many nations when he was already advanced in years. Moses led the Israelites out of Egypt in his old age. These stories remind us that God's timing is perfect, and His purposes for us are always relevant, regardless of our age. Every season of life brings unique wisdom, experience, and opportunities that can be used for His glory. Embracing a new journey in faith isn't just about starting over; it's about continuing to walk on the path God has laid out for us, trusting that He will equip us with everything we need to succeed.

Through my writing, podcasts, and various resources, my aim is always to offer insights and practical advice to empower you to live with intention and purpose. Whether in leadership, writing, podcasting, business, marriage, or parenting, I believe faith should be the cornerstone of all our endeavors.

Want to dive deeper? Here are a few resources I've created. From my podcasts that inspire and challenge listeners to stand firm in their faith, to the Spark Media platform that empowers Christian content creators, each resource is designed to help you navigate the complexities of life with courage and conviction. My hope is that these resources will not only equip you with the tools you need to succeed but also inspire you to take action in your own life. Whether you are leading a team, raising a family, or stepping out in faith to embark on a new venture, remember that God is with you every step of the way. As you explore these resources, I pray that they will strengthen your resolve to live out your faith boldly and purposefully, making a lasting impact in the world around you.

## Podcasts

The *It is Time to Stand Up* podcast is a platform designed to inspire Christians to stand firm in their faith amidst today's challenges. Each episode tackles current issues, cultural obstacles, and personal stories that resonate with believers called to make a difference. My goal is to encourage listeners to stay grounded in their convictions, act courageously, and trust God's guidance as they navigate life's complexities. This podcast is more than just talk; it is a call to action, urging Christians to rise and make an impact in their communities, churches, and beyond. Through interviews, scriptural reflections, and practical advice, *It is Time to Stand Up* empowers its audience to live out faith boldly and purposefully, with truth and love, instilling a sense of responsibility to create a positive impact.

You may also be interested in my other shows: *By His Grace, Spark Influence,* and *Spark Media Conversations.* The *By His Grace* podcast is a faith-centered show where I share personal stories, interview inspiring guests, and provide practical insights to help listeners navigate life's challenges with grace and faith. The podcast focuses on themes such as overcoming adversity, walking in faith, and finding purpose in everyday life. On the *Spark Influence* podcast, my husband Peter and I explore leadership, faith, and personal growth, emphasizing the importance of using one's influence to positively impact others while staying true to one's faith.

The *Spark Media Conversations* podcast is a show dedicated to empowering Christian podcasters and content creators. The podcast features interviews with industry experts, thought leaders, and successful podcasters who share their experiences, insights, and tips on creating impactful content. The podcast covers a wide range of topics, including podcasting strategies, audience growth, branding, and effectively sharing your message with the world.

## Leadership & Speaking

My approach to leadership is grounded in faith, as seen in how I managed Spark Media, a platform dedicated to empowering Christian podcasters. Before establishing Spark Media, I sought God's direction through prayer, asking for His guidance every step of the way. This intentional alignment with God's will guides my leadership and serves as a testimony to the power of faith-driven leadership.

Even though my work with Spark Media has concluded, as an experienced speaker, I frequently lead workshops, conferences, and events. I love sharing my expertise on podcasting, leadership, faith, and business while encouraging women to embrace their God-given purpose.

## Writing

Writing is an extension of one's spiritual journey, crafted to inspire and uplift others. In my writing, I encourage blending creativity with faith. In award-winning *The Struggle is Real: But So is God*, I discuss how my faith has influenced every area of my life, helping me to stand firm and overcome every trial I've faced with the help of the Lord. The Bible Study provides the tools and resources from Scripture to help you know what God says about you and how you can live a victorious life.

I wrote the Spark Media Planner to provide Christian podcasters with a comprehensive tool to effectively organize, plan, and execute their podcasting goals. Recognizing the unique challenges that podcasters face, especially those looking to integrate their faith into their content, we designed the planner to help creators stay on track, manage their schedules, and maintain consistency in their podcasting efforts.

The planner serves as a practical resource, offering structured layouts for planning episodes, tracking goals, and managing tasks, all while encouraging users to align their work with their faith and purpose. By creating the Spark Media Planner, my goal is to empower podcasters to not only grow their platforms but also to make a lasting impact through their content.

I pray these resources encourage you to boldly step into your calling and lead with boldness, purpose, and passion. All of these resources can be found at MistyPhillip.com.

Let me leave you with this encouragement: your life is uniquely designed for this moment in history. God has equipped you with gifts, talents, and a calling that only you can fulfill. You are not here by accident. Your influence—whether in your home, workplace, church or community—can spark transformation and ignite others to step into their own callings.

*God has equipped you with gifts, talents, and a calling that only you can fulfill.*

This is your time to rise up with boldness, fueled by faith, to shine the light of Christ in a world that desperately needs hope and truth. Remember, God does not call the equipped; He equips the called. So, lean into His strength, trust His timing, and walk in obedience, knowing that He goes before you.

As you boldly step forward, may your journey inspire others to do the same. Together, we can create a ripple effect of faith and courage that glorifies God and points countless others toward Him. Stand firm, friend, and let your light shine brightly. The world is waiting. The Kingdom of God is advancing—one obedient, faith-filled step at a time. Let's go and live boldly for His glory!

# PRAYER

*Heavenly Father,*

*Thank You for the calling You have placed on each of our lives. We ask for Your strength and boldness as we step into this calling with passion and purpose. Guide our steps, Lord, and help us to walk in Your ways, staying in step with Your Spirit every day.*

*May our lives reflect Your glory, and may our boldness inspire others to discover and walk in their own callings. Help us to trust You in every season, knowing that Your plans for us are good and perfect.*

*Ignite a passion within us that cannot be extinguished. Use us mightily for Your kingdom.*

*In Jesus' name, we pray. Amen.*

# Appendix Resources

## Activity

### Crafting Your Mission Statement

Now that we've explored how to build a foundation of faith in your business, it's time to put these principles into practice. A mission statement is a powerful tool that captures the essence of your business and communicates your vision to others. For a Christian business, this statement should also reflect your faith and commitment to honoring God in your work.

## Steps to Write Your Mission Statement:

- ✦ Reflect on Your Purpose.
- ✦ Define Your Why.
- ✦ What is the core purpose of your business or your life?
- ✦ How does your faith influence this purpose?

## Identify Key Values

- ✦ What values guide your business decisions?
- ✦ How do these values align with biblical principles?

## Consider Your Impact

- ✦ What impact do you want your business to have on your customers, employees, and community?
- ✦ How can your life and business be a testimony to God's goodness?

## Draft Your Statement

- ✦ Combine your purpose, values, and impact into a concise statement.
- ✦ Make sure it is clear, memorable, and reflects your faith.

## Review and Refine

- ✦ Share your draft with trusted advisors or mentors for feedback.
- ✦ Refine it until it captures the heart of your business and your commitment to God.

## Building on the Rock

Building a business is much like building a house—it requires a strong foundation, careful planning, and ongoing maintenance. As we've explored in this chapter, the foundation of faith is not just an optional component; it is the bedrock upon which everything else must be built. Without it, our efforts are like a house built on sand—vulnerable to the shifting tides of circumstance and time. But when our business is rooted in Christ, guided by His wisdom, and aligned with His values, it becomes unshakable, able to withstand any storm.

Faith is the anchor that keeps us grounded when the winds of uncertainty blow. It is the compass that directs our decisions, ensuring they align with God's will. By integrating faith into every aspect of your business, you not only honor God but also create a legacy that will endure. As you continue your entrepreneurial journey, let faith be the rock on which you build, knowing that with God as your foundation, your business will stand strong, bless others, and ultimately glorify Him.

# Notes

# Assessments

## Assess Your Gifts and Strengths

Consider the unique gifts and strengths that God has given you. How can these be used in your leadership roles? Write about how you can use these gifts to serve others and advance God's Kingdom.

## Personal and Professional Assessments

Here's a list of assessments you can use to evaluate your gifts and strengths, particularly with a focus on personal, professional, and spiritual growth:

## Spiritual Gifts Assessment

Identifies your unique spiritual gifts as outlined in the Bible. Helps align your spiritual strengths with your purpose and calling.

## StrengthsFinder (CliftonStrengths)

Identifies your top strengths from a list of 34 talent themes. Provides insights into how to leverage your strengths in personal and professional settings.

## DISC Personality Assessment

Analyzes your personality based on four traits: Dominance, Influence, Steadiness, and Conscientiousness. Offers insights into how you interact with others and approach tasks.

## Myers-Briggs Type Indicator (MBTI)

Identifies your personality type based on preferences in four areas: Extraversion/Introversion, Sensing/Intuition, Thinking/Feeling, and Judging/Perceiving. Helps understand how your personality influences your behavior, decision-making, and interactions.

## Enneagram Assessment

Categorizes you into one of nine personality types, each with its own strengths and weaknesses. Encourages self-awareness and growth by exploring motivations and fears.

## Emotional Intelligence (EQ) Assessment

Measures your ability to recognize, understand, and manage your own emotions, as well as the emotions of others. Essential for effective leadership, communication, and relationship-building.

## Leadership Practices Inventory (LPI)

Assesses your leadership behaviors and provides feedback on how to enhance your leadership effectiveness. Focuses on practices like inspiring a shared vision, enabling others to act, and modeling the way.

These assessments can help you gain a deeper understanding of your strengths and gifts, allowing you to align them with your personal and professional goals.

www.ingramcontent.com/pod-product-compliance
Lightning Source LLC
Chambersburg PA
CBHW070241010526
44107CB00041B/1484/J